The Doubling Down Trend

A Look Into the Behaviorism of Extreme Risky and Destructive Ideas

By Oscar Xuxa

By reading this document, the reader agrees that under no circumstances is the author responsible for any losses, direct or indirect, that are incurred as a result of the use of the information contained within this document, including, but not limited to, errors, omissions, or inaccuracies.

Table of Contents

Introduction

The individual has always had to struggle to keep from being overwhelmed by the tribe. If you try it, you will be lonely often, and sometimes frightened. But no price is too high to pay for the privilege of owning yourself. - Rudyard Kipling

In an interview conducted by Arthur Gordon with famed author Rudyard Kipling in 1967, Kipling states very plainly that being non-conformist within a society is both immensely difficult and liberating in equal yet opposite measures. Conformity is the act of matching one's beliefs to the most commonly held norms and values within a collection of people.

This can be manifested in both positive and negative outlets. On one hand, within any collective, the desire to live peacefully and to not rock the boat is a reasonable one. On the other hand, it is an exercise in delusion and suppression of the self in order to allow the collective to thrive. The human condition is an incredibly unique state of existence where every individual is special and different in their own way. Allowing that identity and humanity to be suppressed in the interest of convenience and external validation is not only a betrayal against ourselves, but it's also a betrayal against everyone who loved us for who we were.

The philosopher Thomas Hobbes wrote an entire book about how we have certain responsibilities to the society we live in because we owe it to the society for allowing us to live in it. Hobbes believes that a society is formed through a number of people bonded through their shared desire to stay alive and work together to ensure they don't die. In return for the safety provided by society, we are expected to follow the rules of the collective since they are put in place to ensure our protection.

On a fundamental level, conformity would be preferable since synchronized values would ensure that very few conflicts of interest would arise and there would be no compromise of the collective in the case of disagreement. If at any point we do not accept the rules set in place, we can leave that society and choose to live in a secluded cabin, isolated and alone for the rest of our days, which according to Hobbes, wouldn't be a particularly long time.

And even if you don't believe in the post-apocalyptic Mad Max-esque vision of survival that Hobbes has, there's no denying that individuals who run counter to the social and ethical norms of the collective are often ostracized, ridiculed, and mistreated by their contemporaries.

One only needs to look at individuals like Julian Assange, Kanye West, and Vincent Van Gogh to find recognizable examples. Whether their actions and words are justified in the bigger picture or not is irrelevant. What matters with regards to their conduct is that they acted or are acting in a way that ran counter to the social conventions of their time and as a result, were ostracized by an incredible number of their peers.

Imagine this, you are a young teenager who is terrified of not fitting in and not making friends. You would do anything to find a group that likes you and wants you around. Would that mean bullying someone your group is tormenting? Would it mean turning a blind eye to it? Would it mean pulling mean pranks? Would it mean experimenting with dangerous substances when you're not ready to deal with them? None of these scenarios are unimaginable to us, because we were all once a scared kid who wanted to fit in and be loved, and we would go to incredible lengths to find that love. That's what makes conformity so dangerous. The fact that we would go to any lengths to find love that we so desperately want, but feel we need to be inauthentic to ourselves to receive.

Chapter 1: Understanding Conformity

As stated earlier, conformity is a kind of social influence defined by Kassin as "the tendency to change our perceptions, opinions, or behaviors in ways that are consistent with group norms" (Kassin, 2013). Group norms are rules or conditions which are agreed upon by convention by a particular group. Social Influence is a series of ways in which a person's environment can affect their behavior in order to better adapt to the environment. The psychologist Kelman found three particular forms of conformity exist within human behavioral patterns. The three varieties; compliance, identification, and internalization are categorized by the depth of change each variety brings in the individual.

Compliance is a public kind of conformity while still holding on to one's own norms and beliefs in the pursuit of approval or out of fear of rejection. *Identification* is a wish to conform to a role model like a celebrity or a favorite relative. This is fueled by the attractiveness of the source and a desire to emulate them. Finally, *Internalization* is accepting behavior or beliefs on a deeper level depending on the credibility of the source. This is the deepest form of conformity and can take a significant amount of work to lodge free.

While Kelman's research has greatly influenced modern social psychology, modern psychology has adapted his research to discover two reasons why people would actively, or passively choose to conform. On one hand, there is *informational conformity* which is turning to the group in order to gain reliable information regarding reality, and on the other hand, there is *normative social conformity* which is the assimilation of beliefs in order to have a positive relationship with the other members of the group.

Informational Conformity

Social proof, also known as informational influence, is based on the premise that those around you know more about the situation than you do, and is seen as being particularly important in ambiguous social circumstances where people are unsure about how to behave.

The tendency of big groups to conform can be used to observe the impacts of social influence. In some sources, this is referred to as "the herd behavior." Although formal analysis demonstrates that social proof can lead people to converge too quickly on a single distinct choice, decisions of even larger groups of individuals may be based on very little information. Social proof reflects a rational desire to take into account the information possessed by others.

Uncertainty is the key factor when considering informational conformity. It is driven by an individual not understanding the appropriate behavior within a group and thus looking to other members of the group who may or may not have a greater understanding of the rules of the collective. People frequently refer elsewhere for guidance on appropriate behavior when they are in a position when they are uncertain of how to act. When faced with an unclear setting, we tend to conform because we think that other people's interpretations are more correct than our own and will therefore guide us in making the best decision. And conversely, when a person feels like they are part of a community, they are more likely to assimilate and adapt their behavior to be in line with the group's norms.

One of Robert Cialdini's six principles of persuasion is social proof, which holds that people are more inclined to take specific measures if they can relate to those who have already taken them. One experiment that supports this argument was carried out by researchers who participated in a door-to-door fundraising drive. They discovered that the likelihood of the subsequent donor increases with the length of the donor list. When friends and neighbors of the potential donor were included on the donor list, this pattern became even more obvious. Peer pressure is effective, according to Cialdini's principle, since people are more receptive to persuasion strategies used by their peers rather than their superiors. Thus, an individual would be more likely to conform to a sibling's point of view than a parent's.

An example of this practice is when live audiences laugh alongside laugh tracks when recording popular media. The audience believes that the people laughing are similar to them, and thus are more likely to laugh alongside the audio. Another example is when you're on an airplane and everyone claps when the plane lands. Despite this being remarkably annoying and an apparent celebration of not dying, the greater the number of people who clap, the more likely it is for individuals to join in.

There has been a significant amount of research regarding the informative aspect of conformity. One of the more memorable experiments was based around eyewitness examination. The subjects were individually shown an image of a criminal and then asked to identify him from an image of a police lineup.

The image of the line-up was intentionally kept vague and ambiguous and three fake additional subjects working for the researcher were brought in to wrongly identify the same culprit before the real subject was asked. The results showed that the real subjects would be more likely to conform to the wrong answer when they believed it to be a high-importance scenario as opposed to a low-importance scenario.

Normative Social Conformity

Normative Social Conformity is, as the name suggests, the influence other people have on us when we are looking for their approval or validation. This manner of conformity can range from only assimilating public norms while retaining internal behavior to fully accepting the norms of the group as your own in an exercise of self-delusion. This sort of conduct occurs in the interest of maintaining a social unity. When a majority of people agree on a set of rules and beliefs, that group becomes more stable and cohesive, which will help its longevity. Most political parties embrace this notion through their united policies and manifestos.

In 1955, psychologist Solomon Asch conducted a similar experiment to the line-up referenced earlier. In this test, Asch had candidates judge the similarity of drawn-up lines. Then he used fake candidates to provide clearly false answers to the test and have them perform in front of the real candidates. In the public tests, candidates conformed over 36% of the time the clearly false answers given by the fakes. In the private tests without the fakes, the candidates got the right answer 99% of the time. The difference between the witness test and the line test is that there was no ambiguity in Asch's experiment, the answer was intended to be obvious. However, the social pressure of the false candidates led to the real candidates folding and seeking their approval through the incorrect provision of answers.

A person is under more pressure to conform when the other members of the group unanimously support a norm. However, even a slight interruption from unanimity might result in a reduction in the strength of this behavioral effect. In Asch's study, the participant conformed and gave the incorrect response on much fewer trials when even one other false participant disagreed with the majority and gave the right answer. Participants also had sympathetic feelings for these dissenters.

In some variations of the experiment, Asch had dissenting false candidates rejoin the prevailing view when this happened, the real participants felt more pressure from the group and conformed. Conversely, when the conditions were changed and the dissenting parties left the room, the participants did not feel the same expectation to conform as they had when the formerly dissenting party rejoined the majority, and they made fewer errors than they had in the situation where the false candidates rejoined the other members of the group.

When an individual breaks away from the conventions of a collective, they are often branded as deviants and treated negatively by the rest of the group. In practice, we have seen this occur multiple times in both fictional and non-fictional events. The treatment of Monica Lewinsky following the Bill Clinton Scandal during her internship at Washington D.C is a prime example. After her affair with then US president Bill Clinton, Lewinsky became the target of cyberbullying for years affecting both her personal and professional life. The idea of an individual being ridiculed by the general public and made into a figure of mockery is shocking to many, the average person would never dream of committing that kind of bullying. However, jokes at her expense were made conventional through several media figures ranging from news outlets to professional comedians. With so many figures acting in this way, the public reasoned out that it was acceptable to do so, everyone was doing it after all.

Contributing Factors

Of course, while conformity and other manifestations of social influence aren't something that can be measured accurately, there are a number of circumstances that can either foster or mitigate the likelihood of conformity occurring.

Distinctions by Gender, as frequently established by societal standards and studies conducted, have found discrepancies between how men and women adapt to social influence. For instance, Alice Eagly and Linda Carli discovered in their research that women are more conforming and impressionable than men in scenarios involving group pressure under observation. According to Eagly's hypothesis, this discrepancy may be the result of the various gender roles in society. Men are typically raised to be more assertive, whilst women are typically trained to be more compliant.

Additionally, it has been discovered that the gender makeup of the group's structure also affects conformity. In a different series of experiments, conducted by Reitan and Shaw, it was discovered that when participants of both sexes were present, men and women conformed more than when group members of the same gender were present.

Although conformity expectations often rise as the size of the group does, Asch's experiment showed that beyond a factor of three, group size increases had no further effects. In their 1997 study, Brown and Byrne suggested one rationale for this, namely people would suspect collaboration when the majority is greater than three or four.

In addition, a study contends that the impacts of group size are contingent on the social influence moderating the situation. This implies that conformity will be motivated by normative social reasons in circumstances where the group is obviously mistaken; the individuals will conform to be admitted into the group. When the first person responds incorrectly, a participant might not feel any pressure to conform.

However, when each subsequent group member provides the same inaccurate response, the pressure to conform will grow and a person will become more inclined to conform to the group the larger the majority. The less confusing the task or choice, the more probable it is that someone will follow the group's rules. People are less under pressure to comply with rules when duties are unclear. Work difficulty also boosts conformity, but studies show that conformity rises when the task is crucial as well as challenging.

Numerous additional social and environmental elements have been discovered to influence compliance. Accountability makes people more likely to adhere to the group's choices. If someone is attempting to fit in with a group that has specific preferences, they are more likely to conform in order to match those preferences. Another contributing factor is the vagueness/clarity of the decision. The less confusing the task or choice, the more probable it is that someone will follow the group's rules. People are less under pressure to comply with rules when duties are unclear. Work difficulty also boosts conformity, but studies show that conformity rises when the task is crucial as well as challenging.

According to research, people feel more pressure as soon as they realize they don't agree with the majority, which makes them more likely to follow the group's recommendations. Similar to how responses must be given face-to-face, people start to conform more and more. As a result, conformity within a group rises as the anonymity of its members during decisions declines. When individuals have already committed themselves to a group, conformity also rises. After all of the false candidates had openly admitted their replies in a different iteration of the Asch study, the participant was given the opportunity to secretly record his response; this variation of the experiment resulted in a lower degree of participant conformity. In addition, the Asch study's control condition showed that participants' independent responses were virtually always accurate.

Cohesiveness has also been demonstrated to be related to conformity. Research shows that conformity rises as group cohesiveness does because cohesiveness defines how closely members of a group are emotionally bound together. Similar to cohesiveness, conformity is also higher when people want to stay in the group. Additionally, conformity is higher when people are experiencing anxieties stemming from issues with their self-identity; in these circumstances, people are more prone to follow the decisions of the majority.

Minority Influence

Conversely, conformity doesn't always occur through a larger group imposing their conventions on smaller ones. This is unprecedented because it seems to run counter to the social impact theory established by Bibb Latané.

Social impact is described as any effect that others' actual, suggested, or imagined presence or activities have on a person's emotions, thoughts, or conduct. It is the product of social forces such as the strength of the source of impact (a culmination of all the individual qualities that make an individual impactful), the immediacy of the event (how recently the event occurred and whether there were any intervening factors), and the number of sources imposing the impact. The theory states that the impact created by an individual is directly related to the number of sources imposing the impact thus creating the impression that the majority would always be able to impose their norms onto a minority due to its greater volume. This is not the case though when minorities manage to influence their environment.

Social influence comes in two varieties: majority influence (which promotes conformity and outward compliance) and minority influence (resulting in internalization). Majority influence is when the majority tries to make the minority comply, whereas minority influence is when the minority persuades the majority to embrace their way of thinking. A minority member of a group can persuade the majority to agree with their opinions or behaviors. This is known as minority influence. This happens when a select minority or a single person serves as a catalyst for social change by challenging accepted social norms and putting forward fresh, innovative ideas that go against them. Examples of Minority Influence in history are the Civil Rights Movement that dominated the 20th Century within the United States and the dismantling of Apartheid in South Africa.

A majority's influence is viewed as a normative social influence since, as demonstrated by Asch's research, it frequently results from wanting to fit in and conform to the group. A minority position, on the other hand, stands out more, drawing attention and initiating a process of validation in which individuals carefully consider the differences between their own beliefs and the minority's position. This frequently leads to attitude conversion, when the person comes to believe the minority viewpoint—which is much more able to be accepted privately than publicly—is true. The majority influence happens when individuals adopt particular attitudes and behaviors in order to win the approval of others.

The minority group would employ the usage of informational social influence to persuade the majority The majority is drawn in to evaluate and thoroughly study the minority's point of view when fresh or unexpected information is presented that the general populace cannot be certain of nor expect. Following consideration, there is a greater likelihood that the majority group will accept or partially accept the minority perspective when it believes the minority's viewpoint to have more legitimacy and worth.

If the minority's viewpoints is consistent, adaptable, and appealing to the majority, minority influence is more likely to carry over. Consistency and unshakeable conviction will make a position more appealing to the majority, increasing the likelihood that the majority will accept the minority viewpoint. However, if the minority group's beliefs change, the majority could reject their arguments and viewpoints. According to

Serge Moscovici and Charlan Nemeth, minority influence is successful when there is persistence across time and consensus among the minority's constituents. The minority would lack legitimacy if this regularity disappeared.

Even while the majority group could agree with some or all of the minority's viewpoint, this does not always mean that the majority has really been entirely swayed by the minority. According to research by Elizabeth Mannix and Margaret Ann Neale, having the backing of the leader of the majority might prove to be a crucial element in ensuring that the minority perspective is heard and taken into consideration. The backing of a leader increases the minority's credibility in the eyes of the majority, which fosters admiration for the community. The reputation that has been established as a result of the pivotal parties' consistent actions and beliefs is what gives them their power. Because the general populace is more receptive to hearing from people they respect and trust, including important individuals, will assist the minority viewpoint. In minority influence, a few powerful leaders can sway the dissenting mass to the minority's frame of mind. The notion of Authority holding power over the capacity to induce conformity of a population is something that has been researched thoroughly and the findings of such research have been cemented in media and history in a manner that will ensure its longevity far longer than anyone could ever imagine.

Chapter Conclusion

Understanding the building blocks of what conformity consists of is integral in order to understanding what comes next.

Human interaction is beautifully nuanced and complex to the point where massive concepts can go unnoticed by even the most observant of modern detectives. When observing an interaction, understanding the context behind it can be the key to fully comprehending the implications behind an action and making a judgment from it.

Chapter 2: Herd Behavior and Related Concepts

Much like the way we interact with other people differs depending on the situation, conformity can manifest itself in vastly different ways depending on our own interactions with others. There are certain phenomena that collectively affect us yet we are completely unaware of their effects. One of my favorite examples of a widespread effect that we still don't entirely understand is the Mandela effect. The Mandela effect is when a demographic collectively holds a false memory of something which never existed. The term was coined after a large group of people erroneously believed that Nelson Mandela had died sometime in the '80s when he did not actually die until the 21st Century. The likelihood of thousands of people misremembering such a specific detail as the death of an influential politician or misquoting *The Empire Strikes Back* is incredibly fascinating and a little worrying. This chapter is meant to explore other related concepts and their effect on the human psyche.

Memory Conformity

Memory conformity, sometimes referred to as social contagion of memory, is the process whereby memories or information shared by others has an impact on an individual and is assimilated into their memory. Memory conformity is a mistake in memory brought on by both social and cognitive factors. Normative influences, information influences, and source monitoring mistakes are the three varieties of social influence that can cause memory conformity and social contagion errors.

If people think that the source of their knowledge had more time to examine the content, better view, or displayed a high degree of certainty in their judgment, they are more inclined to follow along. According to one study, those with high perceived power are more likely to have an impact on others with low perceived power. High-power persons are more inclined to speak out and take the lead in conversations, whereas low-power folks would often follow and rely on the more assured personality.

One particular study looked at the impact on memory conformance when participants were required to talk about information that was missing, altered, or in direct opposition to what had initially been encoded. According to researchers, the uncertainty and disagreement that arose during trials regarding the verification of additional information provided by a different person assured them that they had missed specific information, probably because of a lapse in attention, which eventually resulted in distorting their memory report. The informational influence was thought to have contributed to the greater volume conformity seen in this experiment because participants were motivated to be precise in their reporting.

A different experiment looked into the verbal elements that affected or predicted memory conformity, especially in terms of the sequence of participant answers. The study demonstrated that the first participant to report a recollection detail was less likely to succumb to social influence, even when the recollection was challenged by another participant. In contrast, even if the memory account differed in detail from what they had personally observed, the person who did not bring up a particular detail initially was more likely to be swayed and subsequently describe what their counterpart had seen.

Famous instances of social interaction, like eyewitness testimony, can serve as examples of alterations of false memories. Memory conformance research has shown that such suggestibility and source monitoring mistakes have far-reaching effects, with significant legal and societal repercussions (Wright et al., 2000).

False testimony resulting from eyewitness mistakes is the most frequent reason for innocent persons being wrongfully convicted. After seeing a crime, eyewitnesses may learn post-event details. There are three main categories of post-event information, the first of which is due to how a leading question may affect how an eyewitness remembers the incident. The second type is when the events that the eyewitness saw are repeated. False information that is present in the recounting is frequently ingrained into the minds of the eyewitnesses, changing their understanding of what actually happened. The third kind of post-event data comes from discussions with other people. They are most vulnerable to external influences muddying their account of the events at this point.

When the witnesses are acquainted with one another, the effects of witness discourse on memory are considerably increased. Regardless of whether the information is real or misleading, people are more inclined to believe it if it is from a trusted confidant. Due to several factors, including a higher level of trust and familiarity in the connection, this individual may be seen as having more credibility than a complete stranger. This type of pattern fits into a wider trend where memory compliance is significantly influenced by the perceived legitimacy of the source of external information.

The possibility that someone will display memory conformity depends in part on how witnesses recollect memories. Studies have indicated that individuals showed greater degrees of subjectivity and significant mistakes in free recall when asked to explain their recollection of a violent crime film in terms of their emotions. Around 43% of participants in a recent research remembered an incident from their childhood that they had never actually experienced (Wade et al., 2014). These inadvertent autobiographical recollections might range widely in time, from current occurrences to early memories. These recollections are comparable to actual childhood memories and have weak sensory detail, which helps the person believe them to be true.

Source Monitoring

When I was a teenager, I once had a dream that I went to my local McDonald's and lost my pants in the kids' area and left after spilling a McFlurry all over myself. When I woke up in sweat, you could imagine my relief that it was just a dream. And relieved I was. Until I noticed my pants were still missing, I had chocolate all over myself and I was sleeping on the bench of a bus stop. Turns out I was just horrifically drunk and what I thought was a harmless dream was actually the very death of my dating life.

The deliberate attempt to ascertain the origin of a memory or piece of knowledge is known as source monitoring. These are frequently one's own interactions with each other and the external world, as well as one's own fantasies and imagination. Which of the choices is the most likely source is determined by the specific and vivid features inside each of them. This information often concerns the location and activities that took place nearby for one's outward experience. These are then compared to other past occurrences in order to determine what the cause could have been. One way to tell if a piece of knowledge comes from fact or fiction is to distinguish between details and vivid details.

An erroneous internal attribution of a memory—the assumption that a memory was formed from first-hand experience—can be caused by a source-monitoring mistake when the information really originated from an external source. Because there aren't enough contrasts between two pieces of information or memories of an event to allow for a clear separation between them, it's likely that the information may be confused and retained erroneously when they have comparable traits. When referring to sources, this could result in inaccurate attributions. An example of this is how it would be more difficult to ascertain who said what in a conversation between identical twins of the same gender, but it would be significantly easier between two siblings of different genders.

Whether a memory inaccuracy or incorrect source attribution happens can be greatly influenced by suggestions and the judgments of others. Legal studies have found that participants around 50% of the time incorrectly ascribed their recollection to a social source, which can exacerbate source-monitoring mistakes. Examples of mistakes in source monitoring have been drawn from actual occurrences, particularly those involving criminal investigations or terrorist activities. Research using the crash of an Israeli airliner in Amsterdam was conducted to demonstrate this. When asked where they had heard about the incident, several people gave bogus information as their source. Although the event had not been recorded on camera, the majority claimed to have watched it on television.

Emotional Contagion

Have you ever been at a concert and feeling a little lethargic and clearly not ready to enjoy yourself when suddenly the performance starts and you feel yourself being reenergized by the artist and in a completely different mood from your initial one? Then you may have caught both the dancing bug as well as emotional contagion.

The spontaneous transmission of emotions and associated actions is referred to as emotional contagion, which is a type of social contagion. It is described as *"a process in which a person or group influences the emotions or behavior of another person or group through the conscious or unconscious induction of emotion states and behavioral attitudes"* by some academics. Such emotional convergence can occur between individuals or within a broader population. People can communicate their emotions to one another in a variety of ways, either directly or implicitly. Personal connections benefit from emotional contagion because it promotes emotional synchronicity amongst people. Early studies claimed that emotional contagion could be explained by conscious thought, analysis, and imagination; nevertheless, some more basic emotional contagion is far more subtle, instinctive, and universal.

It must be noted people's personal emotions were more impacted by the nonverbal cues that other people gave away about how they were truly feeling. One strategy to prevent emotional contagion is to acknowledge your feelings and their source. The reasons for emotional transference have been examined in a wide range of contexts and circumstances, with social and physical factors accounting for the majority of the studies. Emotional contagion has been examined in organizations in addition to the social environments mentioned above. According to researchers, corporations, like civilizations, have "emotion cultures" that include languages, customs, and meaningful cultural practices, as well as guidelines for the emotions and behaviors that employees should and should not exhibit. They claim that "emotion climate," sometimes referred to as morale, organizational morale, and corporate morale, and "emotion culture" are fairly comparable.

In comparison to other modes of communication, emotional contagion tends to be less deliberate and more automatic. Although emotional contagion may and can happen via telecommunication, it mostly relies on nonverbal communication. People communicating via e-mail and chat, for instance, are impacted by each other's emotions without being able to visibly identify non-verbal indications.

According to one theory put forth by certain academics, emotional contagion is a basic, automatic, and unconscious process that happens in a sequence of phases. A receiver notices the emotional responses of a sender when they are conversing. These emotional gestures are instantly imitated by the receiver. These new expressions are translated into experiencing the feelings that the sender experiences through the process of direct feedback, which results in emotional convergence.

A different perspective, originating from social comparison theories, regards emotional contagion as requiring more conscious thought and cognitive effort. This theory holds that people use social comparison to determine whether their emotional response is consistent with others around them. The emotion serves as a sort of social information that the recipient may use to understand how they should be feeling. Positive and negative stimuli generate various reactions from people; negative events often elicit greater and quicker responses than positive or apathetic occurrences. Therefore, negative emotions have a higher chance of spreading negative moods than positive ones. The intensity with which the emotion is communicated is another factor.

The same emotional stimulus (pleasant or unpleasant) stated with high energy would likely cause greater contagion than if communicated with low energy because higher energy draws more attention to it.

In addition to the above-described automatic infection of sentiments, there are instances in which a person or a group would manipulate the emotions of others in order to further their own goals. A leader or team member's deliberate emotive impact may be to blame for this. If this individual were trying to persuade others of something, he may succeed by engulfing them in his excitement. In this scenario, his happy sentiments are an act meant to "contaminate" the sensations of the others.

Collectivism

The predisposition to see oneself as interdependent and a part of a community rather than as an autonomous entity is known as collectivism. This inclination exists both on an individual and social level. People in collectivist societies have a sense of belonging to bigger in-groups or collectives that look out for them in return for their allegiance. Collaborative behavior, communalism, positive interdependence, and adherence to social duties and standards are valued in collectivist cultures. It is especially likely that a collectivist society will place a strong emphasis on the value of respect, social peace, and community needs over individual wants.

There are four key cultural characteristics of collectivism. First, the concept of the individual as interdependent—in terms of others rather than in terms of the impersonal characteristics of an individual. Additionally, the individual must make decisions that take into account the needs of the group and what they are contributing to or taking away from it. This is referred to as an alignment of personal and communal aspirations. Thirdly, while making decisions, societal standards should be taken into account more so than personal preferences. Finally, even if it is bad for people—focus on relationships.

Due to these cultural characteristics, civilizations are fragmented into ingroups. While it is expected that a particular person will only belong to a small number of ingroups, ingroup dynamics and intimacy are closer than in individualistic civilizations. The core tenet of collectivism is that people are bound by organizations and by mutual obligations. Therefore, collectivists place high importance on safety, positive interpersonal connections, synchronicity within ingroups, and individualized partnerships.

The majority of people in North America and Europe have a separate conception of the self as an object that is distinct, independent, self-contained, and equipped with certain tendencies. However, in a vast portion of Asia, Africa, and Latin America, individuals have a mutually dependent view of the individual as a component of a wider social network that also includes family, friends, and those with whom we are socially related. As a result, whereas non-Eurocentric cultures are more prone to feel "other-focused" emotions that foster social peace, Americans and Europeans are more likely to show envy, pride, and other "ego-focused" emotions that establish the self as an independent entity. By the end of the millennium, collectivism was practiced by around 70% of the world's population. Those with lesser levels of income often have more collectivist cultures, whereas countries that experience significant economic growth tend to have more individualistic cultures.

Collective behavior can occasionally be seen in extremely engaged child upbringing. For instance, in Chinese culture, parents and offspring participate in the majority of activities together, and parents are constantly present with their kids, especially if they are under five. As a result, it is advantageous for a kid to reside with senior parents or pay them regular visits.

Collectivistic societies may have a limited range of appropriate behaviors for any particular circumstance. For instance, the highest-ranking person sits closest to the intriguing object, while the lowest ranking person sits the furthest away, during the traditional Japanese tea ceremony. This uncomfortable position is maintained for almost an hour. Before tea is served to the highest-ranking member, the assembly listens to the unique sounds of hot and cold water dripping. The tea is presented to the member with the next highest rating after they have declined an arbitrary amount of times before accepting. Every member participates in this process of denial, which is strictly governed by conventions that cannot be broken.

The structured rituals of collectivism are vanishing, though, as nations experience fast economic development. This is consistent with an overall reduction in traditional responsibilities, such as Japanese adults looking after elderly people. Within the ingroup, uniformity is valued by collectivists; however, this is not true of outgroups. Contrary to popular belief, people from more collectivist societies are more likely to exhibit anti-conformity than people from individualistic ones. Frager's replication of the Asch conformity experiment, in which participants choose to support or oppose an inaccurate group while comparing the forms of lines, revealed that Japanese participants conformed less than those of US participants, a country with a history of individualism.

Despite the fact that collectivism emphasizes harmony, more recent research on collectivist ingroups demonstrates that its members can be more watchful of one another than those in individualist leaning subgroups, attuned to the immoral intents of others. Due to the interdependence of the members of these groupings, one member's immoral actions may spell doom for the entire group.

Herd Behavior

Whoever called man a social animal, really had no idea just how right he was. Humanity, as a collective, has accomplished some of the most incredible things in the history of our world. With our intelligence, ingenuity, and teamwork, humanity has built some of the world's most awe-inspiring monuments, both ancient and modern. From the mystical legends Hanging Gardens of Babylon to the greatest collection of knowledge within the Library of Alexandria, to the sheer insanity that is a Florida Wall-Mart. But when you pull it away, ignore the invention of penicillin, art, and Black Friday marketing schemes man is very little more than a scared gazelle trying not to die painfully. When faced with the very real threat of danger, we revert to our baser instincts which unfortunately look very familiar to a herd of terrified zebras.

Individuals in a group functioning together without centralized guidance is known as herd behavior. Human-based herd behavior includes but isn't limited to: voting, protests, riots, general strikes, sporting events, religious ceremonies, ordinary decision-making, judgment, and opinion formation. I'm of the opinion that Beyonce's concerts should be their own separate category; however, since there is no academic proof of that being the case, I suppose my genius will have to go unrecognized for just a bit longer.

Modern psychological and economic research has identified herd behavior in humans to explain the phenomenon of large numbers of people acting in the same way at the same time.

"Benign" herding behaviors may occur frequently in everyday decisions based on learning from the information of others, such as when a person on the street decides which book to buy. Suppose you're in a bookshop and two books look equally appealing to you and you don't know which to buy. Now, personally, I would buy both because nothing is better than that new book smell, but that's not always the case. Most people would read the more popular book, the one that book reviews are praising and the book that all the people at their workplace are obsessed with. If we all read books based on merit and literary significance, *Fifty Shades of Grey* would never see the coffee table of any middle-aged housewife. However, popularity sells. The more people who are seen acting a particular way, the more likely they are to induce that behavior in others.

The Milgram Experiment

Stanley Milgram, a psychologist at Yale University, conducted a number of social psychology studies titled the Milgram experiment(s) on compliance with authoritative persons. Men between the ages of 20 and 50 who worked in a variety of jobs and had varying levels of education participated in the study, and their readiness to trust an authority figure who told them to do things that went against their personal moral convictions was measured. Participants were made to believe they were taking part in a separate experiment and that they had to shock a "learner" with electricity when they gave the incorrect response. With each consecutive incorrect response, the fake electrical pulses grew stronger until they reached levels that, if they had been genuine, would have been lethal.

In estimating the conduct of 100 imaginary "teachers," Milgram surveyed 14 psychology majors in their senior year at Yale University. The students believed that only a very tiny percentage of instructors, according to all survey participants, would be willing to administer the maximum voltage. In a separate survey of 40 psychiatrists from a medical college, Milgram found that most participants will give up the experiment after the tenth shock, when the "learner" requests to be released. Only 3.7% of the subjects were supposed to remain after the 300-volt shock when the sufferer refused to respond.

In Milgram's initial series of studies, 65% of volunteers delivered the ultimate, powerful 450-volt shock, and every participant delivered shocks of at least 300 volts. The act of doing so made the subjects uncomfortable, and they showed various levels of stress and anxiety. These symptoms included shaking, stuttering, sweating, and in rare cases, anxious laughter fits or seizures.

Anxious laughing or smiling was clearly seen in 35% of the participants. Each participant interrupted the exercise at least once to voice their doubts. After being reassured by the experimenter, the majority proceeded. Even though it was obvious that they were uncomfortable with the experiment, the participants who declined to deliver the last shocks neither demanded that it be stopped nor exited the room to check on the victim's wellbeing without first getting permission to do so. The first interpretation that Milgram derived from his research is the theory of conformism, which outlines the connection between the individual and the group of reference in general. Decision-making will be delegated to the collective and its structure by a subject who lacks the aptitude or experience to do so, especially in an emergency. Every individual model their conduct after the group.

Three months after the start of the trial for German Nazi war criminal Adolf Eichmann in Jerusalem, the tests started in July 1961 at the bottom of Linsly-Chittenden Hall at Yale University. Milgram created his psychological research to address the million-dollar issue and explain the psychology of genocide "Could it be possible that Eichmann and the other millions of Holocaust collaborators were only carrying out their orders? Would it be accurate to call them collaborators?" (Milgram, 1974). By asserting that the same psychological mechanism is crucially engaged in both his tests conducted and events in Nazi Germany, Milgram directly elicited criticism from the scientific community.

According to James Waller, the Milgram experiment volunteers were informed beforehand that their activities would not cause any long-term bodily harm. However, those responsible for the Holocaust were fully cognizant of the murder, humiliation, and disfigurement of their victims.

The test subjects were not based on prejudice or other prejudices, and they did not personally know their victims. However, during a lifetime of personal growth, the Holocaust offenders showed a profound devaluation of the victims.

Contrary to the Final Solution's creators and implementers, who had a predetermined "objective" in mind, those undergoing punishment in the experiment were not sadistic nor hate-mongers and frequently displayed immense agony and turmoil during the experiment.

The subjects were not given any opportunity to think about the effects of their actions throughout the hour-long trial. While the Holocaust continued for years, there was enough opportunity for a moral evaluation of all parties involved.

Chapter Conclusion

After exploring the building blocks of conformity in the last chapter, we have explored that how the structure of those blocks is used to build up and how seemingly illogical and immoral actions can occur. No society functions in isolation, and by understanding the phenomenon that occurs within a society, we can now move forward with these concepts and understand how such a nuanced and subversive thing as conformity can have colossal footprints on the tenuous agreement known as the social contract.

Chapter 3: Bystander Theory

Kitty Genovese, a 28-year-old bartender from the Kew Gardens district of Queens in New York City, New York, was raped and stabbed outside her apartment building early on March 13, 1964. The New York Times falsely claimed in an article two weeks after the murder that 38 witnesses saw or heard the assault but that no one phoned the police or tried to help the victim. The murder became a fixture of American psychology literature for the following forty years as a result of the occurrence, which spurred research into the phenomenon that would later be called the "bystander effect" or "Genovese syndrome." Significant mistakes in the New York Times report have since been debunked by researchers. However, the bystander effect has remained.

According to the social psychology hypothesis known as the *"bystander effect"* or *"bystander apathy,"* people are less inclined to assist a victim when other people are around. However, if a group is required to complete the task, each member will have a weak sense of responsibility and will frequently shrink back in the face of difficulties or responsibilities. If a single person is instructed to perform a job on their own, their individual feeling of obligation will be potent, and there will be a positive response. Since it was first introduced in 1964, a great deal of study, mostly in the lab, has concentrated on a wide range of topics, including the volume of onlookers, ambiguity, group cohesion, and the distribution of guilt that supports mutual denial.

Hart and Ternace Miethe discovered that a bystander was present in 65% of the violent victimizations in the data using information from the National Crime Victimization Survey

(NCVS). The bulk of these violent victimizations was physical assaults, which had the highest prevalence of them (68%) compared to robberies (49%) and sexual assaults (28%). The majority of victims (48%) said that onlookers' activities were "neither helping nor hurting," then "helping" (37%), "hurting" (10%), and "both helping and hurting" (3%). The victim and witness were strangers in half of the cases which occurred in the evening (Hart & Miethe, 2008).

Research Conducted

After becoming interested in the subject following the Genovese murder in 1964, social psychologists Bibb Latané, John M. Darley, and their team first established and popularized the bystander effect in their lab studies by 1968. One of the most potent and easily repeatable responses in social psychology was the outcome of a series of tests carried out by these researchers. In a normal experiment, the subject is either alone or with a group of other subjects or confederates, AKA "researchers pretending to be fellow subjects." A fake emergency is created, and the researchers note down the time it took people to act, if they act at all. According to these studies, assisting is usually significantly reduced when other people are around.

In one of Latane's trials, participants were either on their own, with someone they knew, or with someone they didn't know while a lady was in distress. When the lady was alone, 70% of the individuals cried out or rushed to aid her after assuming she had tripped and was in pain, but when she was partnered with a stranger, only 40% of the people gave assistance. Three additional studies were conducted by Latané and Darley to examine bystander behavior in non-urgent scenarios. Their findings suggested that it made a difference in how the individuals were approached for assistance. In one scenario, participants asked a passerby for their names. When the students introduced themselves, more individuals responded. In another scenario, the youngsters approached onlookers and requested a dime.

When the student provided a reason, such as claiming their money had been swiped, more individuals (72%) were willing to help than when they just asked for a penny (34%).

Latané and Darley list five features of crises that have an impact on bystanders:

- Emergencies entail either a real, or potential risk of damage.
- Emergencies are unordinary and uncommon.
- Different situations call for different types of emergency action.
- Emergencies cannot be anticipated or planned for.
- Emergency situations call for quick action.

Bystanders experience the following cognitive and behavioral processes because of these five characteristics:

1. **Realize that something is occurring**

- Latane and Darley used Columbia University students to manufacture an emergency in order to test the idea of "reality."

- In order to fill out a questionnaire as they waited for the researcher to return, the students were either placed in a room alone, with two strangers, or with three strangers.

- In order to simulate an emergency, smoke was blown into the room through the ventilation while they were filling out the questionnaire.
- When the participants were working alone, they quickly became aware of the smoke (within five seconds).
- Students that were collaborating with one another took up to 20 seconds longer to detect the gas.
- According to Latané and Darley, this occurrence might be justified by the societal standard of what is seen as proper behavior in public.
- In the majority of western cultures, courtesy implies that it is improper to aimlessly scan the area.
- This can suggest that the individual is rude or inquisitive. Because of this, people on the street are more predisposed to mind their own business in large groups than they are when they are alone.
- A person in need of aid is more likely to be spotted by an individual who is alone since they are more cognizant of their surroundings.

2. Consider the problem as being urgent.

- If a bystander observes a situation and believes it to be an emergency, they may be more likely to step in.
- Bystanders observe other people's responses in an emergency scenario in accordance with the social influence principle to determine if others believe it is important to respond.
- Bystanders will view the issue as not being urgent if it can be ascertained that other people are not responding to it. Social proof, as mentioned earlier, is evident in this situation.
- During the smoke experiment even though the students in the groups had obviously observed the smoke, which had grown so thick that it was obstructing their

- eyesight, hurting their eyes, or inducing coughing fits, they were still unlikely to disclose it.
- By the end of the trial, no one from five of the eight groups had reported any smoke at all. Only one participant in the group setting had identified the smoke within the first four minutes.
- The interpretations of the smoke's source and the possibility that it was actually dangerous were likewise less serious in the groups that didn't mention it; no one suggested fire as a probable cause, although several preferred less grave answers.
- Similar to how context readings influenced people's responses to a man assaulting a woman on the street. Bystanders interfered 65% of the time when the victim was unaware of the attacker, but just 19% of the time when she hinted at being his wife.
- Ambiguity is one of the things that influence whether or not someone helps someone who is in need.
- It can take a person or several people up to five times longer to act when there is high ambiguity than when there is little ambiguity.
- In these situations, onlookers assess their own well-being before moving forward.
- In low ambiguity, negligible consequence scenarios as opposed to high ambiguity, substantial consequence situations, bystanders are more inclined to take action.
- Latané proposed that in confusing circumstances, onlookers can turn to one another for direction and mistake others' lack of an early reaction for indifference.
- Each onlooker concludes that the issue is not serious as a result of this informational influence.

3. Feeling of responsibility

Researchers found that a bystander's sense of responsibility is influenced by three factors: Whether they believe the individual deserves assistance or not; the bystander's capability; and the connection between the victim and the bystander

4. Types of support

- Direct intervention: aiding the sufferer directly
- A detour intervention: The process of notifying the authorities of an emergency.

5. Put the decision into action.

According to a 2011 investigation of the bystander effect, When offenders were present, the costs of involvement were physical, and circumstances were seen as unsafe the bystander impact was reduced. This pattern of results is in line with the arousal-cost-reward paradigm, which postulates that assisting is increased when threatening events are identified more quickly and clearly as genuine crises. In addition, they identified circumstances in which bystanders offer helpful physical support for the potentially mediating individual and thereby reduce the bystander effect.

Another factor that may influence a bystander's tendency to provide assistance is the cohesion of the group. The effectiveness of bystanders in groups of individuals they are familiar with has been tested through experiments. According to the research, helping behavior is influenced by the social responsibility norm. People *"should support those who are in need of help and who are dependent on them for it,"* according to the social responsibility standard.

According to research carried out, a group is more likely to behave in accordance with the social responsibility standard the more cohesive they are. Undergraduate students were utilized as the subjects of an experiment where they were split into four groups: an incohesive group of two, an incohesive group of four, a highly cohesive group of two, and a highly cohesive group of four. The cohesive group then got to know one another by doing introductions, talking about what they enjoyed and didn't like about school, and other related things. The experiment's goal was to find out whether cohesively strong groups were more likely than less cohesive ones to provide a hand to a harmed "victim." The fastest and most inclined groups to react to the victim whom they believed to be wounded were the four members of the highly cohesive groups. Whilst the four members of the incohesive group were the least likely and slowest to provide assistance.

According to studies on the psychological components of the concept of altruism, helpful behavior occurs more frequently when the giver and the recipient share characteristics. The impact of resemblance, and more especially, common group affiliation, in promoting bystander intervention has been examined in a recent study. In a particular study, researchers discovered that spectators were more willing to assist an injured individual if they were sporting a football shirt from their favorite team, as opposed to their least favorite. However, followers of both clubs were significantly more likely to be aided, when compared to a person wearing a plain jersey, when their shared identification as football enthusiasts was made apparent.

According to a 2009 survey by the International Ombudsman Association, there are several reasons why individuals choose not to take immediate action or report improper workplace behavior. The two main reasons given for passive action were a fear of "negative repercussions" and a concern of losing significant connections in and outside of the workplace (Scully

& Rowe, 2009). People who intervened immediately or reported crimes to the police did so for a variety of reasons, as well. The association's research implies that a far broader approach might be used to study and analyze the "bystander impact." The larger perspective takes into account more factors than simply what bystanders do in certain circumstances to assist strangers in need when other individuals are present or not.

Analysis of bystander reactions is also possible when they see a wide range of inappropriate behavior over time, are in a workplace structure and are interacting with known individuals. Numerous factors were cited in the practitioners' research as to why some bystanders inside businesses choose not to intervene or report undesirable behavior. According to the study, bystander conduct is also frequently beneficial in terms of providing immediate assistance and notifying authorities of inappropriate behavior (as well as emergencies.) According to the study, what bystanders would really do in real scenarios is quite complicated, including views of the surroundings, their bosses (and any applicable organizational structures), as well as a variety of personal factors.

Why is the Bystander Effect Harmful?

We all want to believe that somewhere deep down we are worthy and good. We all want to believe that if given the chance to do good and do the right thing, we would instantly realize it and chase it down like the heroes we grew up watching on T.V. Because fundamentally we all believe that we know what the right thing to do in any given situation is.

When I was a child, I didn't understand why the crowd on the subway in *Spider-Man 2* didn't help fight off Doctor Octopus. They knew he was a villain, didn't they? They had to know he was going to hurt everyone on that train unless something stopped him. As I got older, I realized that aside from the four mechanized hydraulic tentacles, there is far more stopping a crowd from intervening.

Stepping up to stop perceived injustice is a net positive, that is something that we can all agree on. But recognizing injustice is a much harder thing to accomplish. I know I wouldn't be able to forgive myself if I was ever in a situation where my intervention, either directly or indirectly caused irreversible harm to someone. Many people would argue that the intention to help is enough, but intentions aren't enough to induce favorable results.

When I was seven years old, I found my mother crying on the kitchen floor. I heard her yelling at someone over the phone and after the call ended, she just collapsed. My seven-year-old mind thought I should make her a cup of hot chocolate; it always made me feel better so it should be good enough for her. Since seven-year-olds aren't nearly as coordinated as they would like to believe they are, I ended up scalding my arm, breaking a ceramic mug in my hand, and rushed to ER in an ambulance. In between the crying and fainting from blood loss, I heard my mother complaining to the paramedic that I ruined her day and I should have just minded my own business. The tone she used... you wouldn't believe she was talking about her injured son; you'd think she was talking about a particularly dim pug who made a mess of the carpet. So, from then on, I did. "Keep your head down and don't rock the boat" was my catchphrase during the early stages of puberty. "Don't muck things up, Boy" was my mother's.

When I turned 16, I met someone who I now consider to be an older sister. Spending everyday after school doing homework at her apartment made me feel so mature, like a real adult. But I also had my doubts. Why would a 20-something college student want to spend time with a kid? Would I start drinking? Would I be forced to take drugs? The truth, depending on your opinion of public speaking, was arguably worse. Turns out, she was the mentor of a youth activism program and thought that I would benefit from an extracurricular that demanded I take a stand and defend something I believe in. Fast forward multiple years, and I end up taking over the program and going around high schools giving kids the same exact spiel I received.

That program and my friend taught me a lot of things. There is always a good way to approach an issue, but hindsight is 20/20. After an issue has passed, it's always easier to nitpick what went wrong and how you could have done better. That fear of making things worse shouldn't stop anyone from acting though. If you never start a car, how would you be able to know if there's a problem with the engine? Every single one of us has a basic enough understanding of conventional morality to know when something isn't right. Taking a stand for that belief isn't being impulsive, it's having integrity. On a macro-level, society has only ever thrived as much as it has through the very human desire to make things better. Why can't we embody that on a micro-level too? Everyone has a hill that they're willing to die on, and sometimes all that can be done is to fight the good fight and go down swinging. Actively interfering with unjust acts is something that only takes one person to induce. The experiments shown earlier indicate that the bystander effect is significantly weaker if at least one person is willing to go against the tide. We should all aspire to be that one person and be the drop in the ocean that causes a ripple.

Chapter Conclusion

On October 24, 2009, a female student at Richmond High School was lured into a secluded area outside the school's homecoming event where she was gang-raped and brutally attacked by a number of boys and men. Until the attack began, which reportedly lasted over two hours before a young woman called the police, she reportedly received pleasant treatment and drank alcohol with the gang. Up to 20 individuals saw the event, and some of them apparently cheered and recorded it on camera. Injuries from the event resulted in her hips frequently popping out of place, and she was hospitalized for scrapes and bruises all over her body and face. She also subsequently received cigarette burns all over her back.

If what you just read makes you feel deeply uncomfortable, then congratulations, you're not a heartless automaton. That teenage girl was assaulted in the most horrific manner imaginable, and not one of 20 witnesses thought to call the authorities or intervene. One of the witnesses was quoted saying, *"I feel like I could have done something, but I don't feel like I have any responsibility for anything that happened"*. That kind of reasoning makes me deeply uncomfortable as a human being, as a full-grown adult, and as a youth mentor. The idea that I could find out one of my kids was in that position and no one in the immediate vicinity made the choice to help them, is one I deeply loathe. That girl had to undergo one of the most painful experiences any sentient being could go through all because there was not a single person willing to affirm that sexual assault is wrong. That is why the bystander effect is harmful. The idea that a group can sit passively while injustice occurs is one, we, as a society, cannot entertain. None of us are passengers in our own lives, let's not become ones in the lives of others.

Chapter 4: The Psychology and Charisma of Cult Leaders

Charles Manson, Jim Jones, and David Koresh, these three people are select examples of a particular kind of individual, the cult leader. Objectively, a cult is a social group that is *"defined by its unusual religious, spiritual, or philosophical beliefs and rituals, or its common interest in a particular personality, object, or goal"*. That definition can be stretched to refer to any kind of religion. Anyone raised as an atheist can tell you that the idea of a giant man in the sky threatening to spank people for bad behavior is dubious at best. But cults are different. There is a different implicit connotation when we speak of cults. When we speak of cults in the modern day, we do it with the understanding that they employ unconventional and inhumane methods to indoctrinate their members into becoming devoted followers unrecognizable to their friends and family.

There are several subcategories of cults, with destructive cults receiving the most publicity due to their dynamic modus operandus. Cults like the Branch Davidians People's Temple and the Manson Family fall within this category, with the Branch Davidians and Manson Family also qualifying as doomsday cults due to their belief structure. These particular organizations have made their bloody mark on history with the performance of horrific acts of depravity upon their own members and outsiders in equal measure.

Steven Hassan in his book cites the BITE model as the main method cults use to enforce their wills unto their followers.

His BITE model states that if a harmful cult is successful in controlling one or more aspects, the rest will often follow. In contrast to brainwashing, Hassan describes mind control as "a system that interferes with a person's healthy identity development." Beliefs, actions, thoughts, and emotional patterns make up identities. Cults replace this real identity with a false one when they indoctrinate a member. Hassan claims that while this might happen immediately, it often takes a bit longer to happen even if the person first adopts a cult identity to fit in without genuinely adhering to the cult's philosophy. Behavior, information, thinking, and emotion are Hassan's four pillars of mind control. BITE is an acronym for the four types of control a Cult attempts to usurp from their **Behavior**, **Information** received, private **Thoughts**, and individual **Emotions.**

By modifying the external environment, for as by requiring that all members live in a compound together, destructive cults can manipulate behavior. They can also keep their members occupied. Cults can also use sleep deprivation as a means of behavior control by structuring their members' days. Many adherents must get permission from the cult leader in order to escape or contact relatives. Some cults require members to contribute all of their money and other things, leaving them completely dependent on the cult in terms of finances. Praise and punishment are made simple under hierarchical leadership. Instilling pride or making the entire group, including the offending person, realize the necessity for punishment, a higher-up might either laud or denounce a member.

Cults control the dissemination of information to "*rob people of the ability to make informed decisions.*" Cults sometimes achieve this by isolating their members in isolated communes. However, even groups that do not employ physical separation can manipulate information, for example, by demonizing external sources as demonic, false, or propaganda. Cult members are typically given cult propaganda when they do find space to read or think for themselves. Additionally, members are forbidden from criticizing the organization among themselves. Members are instructed to ask for help from mentors and more senior members instead. Contact with outside relatives, friends, and ex-members, in particular, is discouraged since they might best explain whatever the cult has done to the new member.

Internalizing cult theory helps members maintain thought control. Cult teachings are frequently absolutist, rendering all arguments binary and devoid of subtlety. Whatever the charismatic leader does and thinks is the right thing to follow. What others do and think are bad things. Members no longer have to reason independently because cult ideology already clarifies and addresses any queries at the last stage of mental mind control. Cults frequently use their own language as a means of mind control and to distinguish members from outsiders. Take the case of the Unification Church's "Cain-Abel issue." When a group member disagreed with a mentor or higher-up, they were informed it was a Cain-Abel issue and that they (Cain) should submit rather than try to overthrow the leader (kill Abel). The dispute could only be resolved in this way.

Members of destructive cults are often instructed to "block out any information that is critical of the group" throughout their training. Denial, justification, rationalization, and wishful thinking are some examples of this. Thinking stopping is a severe sort of thought control. Members are advised to quit thinking of negative ideas and think only positive, pure thoughts. They "focus themselves" if they consider something negative and filter it out, which keeps members from questioning the cult, especially within their own minds.

Prayer, meditating, singing, etc., are all effective ways to stop thinking. Hassan emphasizes that these activities are not detrimental in and of themselves. When destructive cults utilize them to train members to shun any ambiguity and doubt, they turn dangerous.

It is hard to think adversely about the cult or leader if a member is proficient at stopping their thoughts. Instead, they internalize blame for whatever problems they encounter. Members may become even more motivated as a result. Hassan claims that when a cult has influence over a person's thinking, it nearly invariably also has control over that person's emotions and conduct.

In order to maintain emotional control over their members, cults use feelings of satisfaction, guilt, and terror. Hassan explains how a cult might train individuals to remain by conditioning them to feel great while they are being loyal while feeling guilty or afraid when they make a blunder or rebel by constricting their range of emotions. Guilt may be a result of the past, present, identity, or a social group. When the religious leader calls out their inadequacies, members tend to internalize their guilt and feel more ashamed since many cult members think they are to blame when doctrines sound nonsensical or work. Hassan explains how a double-bind habit, often known as oscillating between praise and condemnation, is a popular cult method to instill powerlessness.

Fear unites groups by first establishing a terrifying external environment in which group members are being persecuted and then by creating a terrifying interior environment in which cult leaders might soon identify and punish a member for being inadequate. For instance, some organizations assert that cult members would bring about the end of the world if they don't labor and believe as hard as they should. To heighten the feeling of terror, other groups employ the mind control technique of having their members spy on one another. Members are scared of leaving or being expelled because of this "phobic indoctrination," believing that if they do, they will lose their minds, get murdered, etc.

Emotions may also be redefined in cults. Hassan talks about a religious sect that claims that happiness comes from a deeper relationship with God. Being miserable and experiencing suffering are essentially the purest forms of bliss, as it is also taught that God is unhappy. Other cults preach that the key to happiness is to submit to the authority of the leader and advance the cult. Public repentance is used to induce guilt and eventually blackmail the group's participants. Despite cults' claims that confessing brings about atonement, members are rarely pardoned, and prior offenses may subsequently be brought up to maintain someone's composure.

Many cults utilize sexuality to their advantage, either by demanding sex and labeling members who refuse greedily or by forbidding it and creating dissatisfaction.

The Manson Family was a religious commune based in an abandoned western movie set fueled by LSD and brought together Charles Manson's magnetic charisma and the cult of personality. Throughout the late '60s to the early '70s the Manson family committed depraved acts of violence against several individuals in Los Angeles resulting in the lifetime incarceration of its leader and several high-ranking members of the cult.

Between 1954 to 1978, an American cult known as the Peoples Temple of the Disciples of Christ, or simply the Peoples Temple, operated. The Peoples Temple, founded in Indianapolis, Indiana, by Reverend Jim Jones, promoted a message that merged Christian doctrine with radical left-wing theory with a focus on racial equality. The People's Temple left its bloody footprints in American history with the events of November 18, 1978, when 909 people perished in a mass suicide and mass murder at its isolated community, called "Jonestown," as did Congressman Leo Ryan and members of his entourage.

The General Association of Branch Davidian Seventh-day Adventists, often known as the Branch Davidians, was an apocalyptic new cult started in 1955 by Benjamin and Lois Roden. In 1981, Vernon Howell, a young man who would eventually go by the name David Koresh, traveled to their headquarters, New Mount Carmel, to study biblical prophecy with Lois Roden. By the end of 1983, Howell had attracted a following, and they broke away from Lois' group to create their own. After starting a bloody civil war, Howell's branch violently took the land that belonged to other sect members and built a new compound. At the end of a 51-day standoff between the sect and federal agents, Koresh's leadership of his group came to an end when New Mount Carmel was completely destroyed in a fire.

Charles Manson: There'll be Helter-Skelter to Pay

Tall, Dark, and Handsome? Cigarette in mouth, Guitar in hand, and a smirk on his lips? If you think I'm describing Johnny Cash, you'd be wrong. Charles Manson, born in 1934 was an American criminal and musician as well as the head of the Manson Family, a cult with its headquarters located in an abandoned Californian movie set, in the late 1960s. His cult of personality and charisma motivated some of the adherents to perpetrate a string of nine murders at four different sites in July and August 1969. In 1971, Manson was found guilty of first-degree murder and conspiring to murder seven people, including eight-month pregnant actress Sharon Tate, former spouse of infamous director Roman Polanski. Because of his purported capacity to exert such a mental grip on others, leading them to commit horrible killings under his sway, as proven by the female members of the family, Manson has stood out as being of unique psychological intrigue and horror.

One of the most challenging mysteries that the field of behavior and personality research has ever attempted to unravel is the motivations behind the cult and the sinister infatuation with Charles Manson. Although Charles Manson is regarded as one of the most terrible people in history, he wasn't a serial killer, it should be mentioned. He was never even linked to classic serial killers like Ted Bundy or John Wayne Gary. The Manson Family is unquestionably one of the most intriguing families ever from a psychological perspective. Based on a highly particular, secret dogma called "Helter Skelter"—named after the Beatles song—Manson urged, persuaded, and coerced his disciples into executing murders.

Although the song was about obstacles in romance, it meant more to him than that. It served as the reason for an impending race conflict between whites and blacks. He was both engrossed with and motivated by it. Over two evenings, all of the offenses were committed. To put this in context, it wasn't an urge and was completely unrelated to any kind of mental illness.

One of the first psychiatrists to discover any justifications for attraction with someone as evil as Charles Manson was Sheila Isenberg. He had fully embraced himself as the "Devil man," shaving his head and beard into a goatee and carving a swastika tattoo into his forehead. In her book *Women Who Love Men Who Kill*, Dr. Isenberg put up a number of distinct psychological hypotheses. In the first justification, "hyper-empathy syndrome" is discussed. Women with extremely low self-esteem exhibit it. They frequently make connections with prominent or well-known individuals who make them feel valued. In this case, their excessive empathy is what makes it possible for them to have a strong connection with the individual. It can even reach the point where they defend the murderer's wicked deeds.

Charles Manson yearned for power, notoriety, and fortune. By establishing a connection with his potential followers and then enticing them into unbalanced and exploitative relationships, Manson took advantage of the drugged-up, free-spirited rebellion of the time.

The key to Manson's control was to make sure that followers saw themselves as members of a superior elite who had the answer to the world's problems—even if that meant the death of the world as they knew it. Manson did this by portraying himself as an omnipotent, high priest-esque figure. His followers found his meandering, incomprehensible apocalyptic worldview to be completely compelling regardless. Manson specifically seemed to target young women and runaways who came from damaged homes and molded them into his own personal harem. He would make himself the center of their world and mold their being around himself like a disturbed potter.

Manson became the center of his followers' life; he met their desires for a "family" and other essentials. With disastrous effects, his "family members" took actions to advance the spiritual aspect of themselves that was connected to him. This may provide an explanation as to why his cult members were able to commit atrocities themselves or witness horrible deeds and take no action to stop them. They would be going against themselves and everything they had placed in Manson if they took action against him. This indicated that they would be faithful to the death if necessary. For the believers, committing these awful atrocities was the height of devotion and confirmed their cult identity. Identical to Joan of Arc being burned at the stake.

Former Manson member Dianne Lake recalls that 10 to 15 members of the Manson family established into the mundane chores of commune living at Manson's commune on Spahn Ranch. These tasks included rummaging through dumpsters for food, caring for horses and every once in a while, renting them out for rides, as well as late-afternoon trips with Manson playing music. The gang would also routinely partake in drug usage and meticulously planned orgies where LSD was administered as a religious ritual.

Manson was basically just a regular misogynist, like a plethora of sociopathic predators whose violence has captivated American culture. He wasn't a part of the 1960s counterculture; rather, he was a brilliant conman of it who preyed on a group of damaged, mistreated young women while in prison using the "free love" attitude of the period. The Manson cult leader gradually took on a major role in the followers' identities and self-esteem. The cult and its leader become the sole reason for the members' existence.

Manson had a strategy, and perhaps more intriguing for the researchers, he encouraged his followers to carry out other killings thereafter. He didn't give them much time to reflect on their actions. He had outstanding manipulative and persuasion skills, so much so that he completely suppressed the emotions and inhibitions of his Family.

Jim Jones: The Road to Jonestown

American cult leader and evangelist James Warren Jones identified himself as a spiritual healer and political activist. Between 1955 and 1978, he was the leader of the Peoples Temple, an American destructive religious group.

Amidst the turmoil of the Civil Rights Movement and Cold War scares from the Soviet Union, mid-twentieth century America was a terrifying place to be in. Rev. Jim Jones emerged from the confusion caused by these societal problems with some revolutionary views that attracted a wide variety of cynical and disillusioned Americans. Jones' fervent criticisms of segregation and the "abuses, disgraces, and inconsistencies of American capitalism," as well as his visions of an ideal society in which everyone was treated equally regardless of their position in the social order, drew in the crowds to Temple services. Jones' magnetic personality and captivating oratory abilities were likewise appealing and convincing. Jones increased his hold over his followers by using this ferocity. In order to increase his control, he persuaded newly initiated

Temple members to sell their possessions and donate their assets to the Temple.

It was initially well-known in Indianapolis for its social action and for helping those who were less fortunate in society through the establishment of a soup kitchen, an orphanage, and service provision for the disabled. The Temple's dedication to societal equality was motivated by Rev. Jim Jones himself with him and his wife being the first white couple to adopt an African American kid in Indiana's history as well as going on to adopt several children of non-caucasian ethnicity. To many, Rev. Jones seemed to be the face of progress and social activism. This rising trajectory did not prove to be sustainable, however.

By the late 1970s, media portrayals of the Temple were starting to depict impressions that were progressively more negative than the ones from its early years. These new depictions presented a picture of a sect that resembled a cult, whose members were forbidden from leaving and isolated from their family and society as a whole. After journalists reported one of Jones' miraculous healing sessions while visiting his former church in Indianapolis in October 1971, Jones started to get bad press.

While Jones' public persona promoted socialism and equality, his interactions with his followers did not reflect these beliefs. Through progressively brutal measures that increased his followers' subservience to the point where they were almost devoid of free will, Jones reshaped the existence of his acolytes while Peoples Temple was in operation.

Jones inflated the idea that he was a Messianic figure in order to openly defend his authority over his followers. He requested that his followers address him as "Father" and employed a number of strategies to demonstrate his divine authority to his flock.

Since his collaborative ventures with William Branham and his Pentecostalists, Jones had been doing "miracles" of faith healing. His healings had often been exposed as being a fraud. Irene Mason, a member of the Temple, was spiked by Jones in one instance, and an arm cast was applied to her while she was out cold. When she woke up, she was informed that she had fractured her arm in the fall and was transported to the hospital. Jones revealed her "recovery" during a following healing session by taking off her cast before the Temple. In other cases, Jones had a member of his inner circle join the cancer prayer line. The individual would then appear to cough up their cancerous tumor after being "healed," which so coincidentally happened to be a chicken gizzard. Additionally, Jones claimed to have "special revelations" about specific people, purportedly exposing previously unknown aspects of their life. In the guise of conducting an unrelated assessment, Jones' followers visited the homes of the prospective recruits and conducted in-depth interviews. This gave Jones access to inside knowledge that would give the impression that he has superhuman abilities and was omniscient.

To avoid the potential of a government raid on their compound, Rev. Jim Jones relocated his sect of several hundred acolytes from San Francisco to Jonestown, a remote agricultural property in Guyana, in 1977. Congressman Leo Ryan and a team of journalists visited Jonestown to look into claims of tyranny and brutality made by relatives of Temple followers under Jones' authority. After Ryan narrowly missed being attacked by a Temple member on November 18, his group hastily departed. Ryan was able to bring along 15 cultists who had expressed a wish to quit. Ryan and several members of his party were shot and killed by Jonestown's Red

Brigade of armed guards under Jones' orders as members of his party boarded two airplanes at the Port Kaituma airfield.

When Jones learned that Ryan's party had not been completely eliminated by his security officers, he came to the conclusion that the survivors would soon alert the US about the attack, and they would dispatch the military to retake Jonestown. Senator Ryan was dead, he told the group, and the military commandos attacking their commune and massacring the Temple was inevitable.

Jones and a few other members made the case that the organization should commit "revolutionary suicide" using that justification. Jones captured the whole funeral rite on audio tape. Jones had brought substantial quantities of cyanide into Jonestown. Flavor Aid and the poison were combined to make a drink that was distributed to community members. The children were the first ones forced to drink the concoction in order to reduce resistance among the parents. "Suicide drills" were performed within the compound to emotionally harden the Temple when faced with the death of loved ones. When the parents realized that this was no longer a drill, most of them lost the will to live and drank the cyanide to join their children in the promised place Jones promised.

However, the recurring mock suicides serve to back up the argument that Jonestown was an unwilling massacre as opposed to suicide because they were just one more tool in Jones' arsenal for mind control. Through theatrics, Jones reduced the seriousness of suicide to an "ever-present reality," making it nearly instinctive for his followers. Many Temple followers were no longer capable of considering leaving or even resisting the thought of suicide at that point due to their extreme physical and mental breakdown. The residents of Jonestown had reached their breaking point. They had been humiliated, beaten, robbed of sleep, treated with contempt, cut off from their loved ones, and deprived of all personal liberties. Those who refused to drink were forcefully injected with cyanide via syringe resulting in 909 casualties, 276 of whom were children. The survivors managed to escape their fates by hiding in the jungle, and the dormitories, and running away from the compound.

The Jonestown massacre was the greatest single loss of civilian life in American History until the events of 9/11. The evil and fanaticism exemplified by Jim Jones still affect many people today. The events of Jonestown were recorded in 45 minutes of footage known as the Death Tape and show the events of the massacre in real-time. Jim Jones was a manipulator and egomaniac whose devotion to God was only ever a smokescreen for his devotion to himself.

David Koresh: Mount Carmel's Last Stand

David Koresh, who came from a troubled family history, was born Vernon Wayne Howell on August 17, 1959, to a 14-year-old single mother. Koresh highlighted the loneliness of his early years. He was a social pariah because of his dyslexia and bad study habits, but he could memorize religious texts very accurately. In 1981, Koresh relocated to Waco, Texas, where he joined the Branch Davidians, a group that was established in 1955 with new beliefs unaffiliated to the original Davidians and was created by the then-deceased Benjamin Roden. Using his affair with Roden's widow, Lois, Koresh climbed the ranks of the Branch Davidians and spread claims that his offspring with Lois would be considered the chosen one by the Lord. Naturally, Roden's existing son George wasn't too thrilled by that.

Koresh and his crew were ejected from the property under the threat of violence by Roden, who claimed to have the backing of the majority of the cult. In Palestine, Texas, 90 miles (140 km) from Waco, Koresh and about 25 followers set up camp. For the next two years, they endured terrible living conditions while traveling to find new recruits. Koresh and his supporters lived in destitution after being banished to the Palestine camp. The exiled Branch Davidians feared they would never be able to return to the Mount Carmel Center after Lois died in 1986, but despite their exile, "Koresh now enjoyed the loyalty of the majority of the [Branch Davidian] community," according to one report.

Roden unearthed at least one cadaver from the local cemetery in 1987. Roden claimed that he was only shifting the cemetery, but Koresh asserted that Roden had challenged someone to raise the dead person from the dead, and that person would then become the next leader. When Koresh went to the authorities to report Roden for forcibly exhuming a corpse, he was informed that he would need to provide evidence. In a purported effort to obtain photographic evidence of the exhumation, Koresh jumped at the chance to return to the Mount Carmel Center with seven armed supporters in order to get his revenge against George Roden. Roden discovered Koresh's crew, and a shootout resulted in Koresh ultimately gaining the spiritual victory and leadership of the Branch Davidians.

David Koresh had memorized the whole Old and New Testaments of the Bible by the time he was 18 years old. He said that he conversed with God, who revealed to Koresh that he was the Messiah and the one who had been chosen. Koresh's ability to persuade others stemmed not just from his charm but also from his in-depth understanding and application of the scriptures. People were astounded by Koresh's reinterpretation of the Book of Revelations when a series of cassettes featuring him analyzing the Bible and explaining how it related to his purpose made their way through various church organizations throughout America.

Koresh's manipulation strategies have a rock-solid foundation in The Book Of Revelations. It's not unexpected that Koresh was able to pervert these teachings into a rigid code of behavior with his own self-interests at its core given that individuals who lived at the compound were initially led there by Koresh's interpretation of this literature and persisted once converted by his goal. Dr. Stephen Diamond, a psychologist, compared Charles Manson's methods to his own by saying that he operated *"by identifying and targeting a vulnerable and needy group of people already seeking a messiah."* His cassettes were a great way to attract his ideal demographic. Dr. Diamond described these people as *"individuals who are susceptible to suggestion and searching for someone to lead them out of what they perceive as Hell and into the Promised Land"* (Diamond, 2006).

Koresh published the "New Light" audiotape on August 5, 1989, in which he claimed that God had instructed him to have children with the group's ladies in order to construct a "House of David" of his "special people." Couples in the group who were married had to consent to be split up in order to allow only him to have sexual intercourse with the wives while the males were to observe abstinence. Newspaper articles dubbed "The Sinful Messiah," additionally claimed that Koresh had physically assaulted minors on the premises and had committed statutory rape by taking numerous underage brides, and started appearing in local news publications on February 27, 1993.

In order to plan for the end of times and the salvation of his followers, Koresh also claimed that God had instructed him to begin assembling an "Army for God." When a UPS carrier informed local law police that a box had burst open on route to the Branch Davidian house, revealing guns, inert grenade shells, and black powder, Koresh and his disciples were suspected of amassing illegal weapons. In May and June of that year, two cases of inert explosives, black gunpowder, 90 pounds of powdered aluminum metal, and 30 to 40 cardboard tubes were reported to the county sheriff.

When the ATF invaded Mount Carmel Center on February 28, 1993, the Waco siege officially started. Six Branch Davidians and four ATF agents were killed in the subsequent gunfight. The FBI Hostage Rescue Team quickly assumed control of the federal operation following the first raid since the FBI has authority over instances involving the killing of federal personnel. A gunshot had caused grievous injuries to Koresh personally. He and his inner circle arranged delays while the standoff went on so that he could draft the holy writings he claimed to need to finish before turning himself in. Koresh's discussions with the negotiators were nuanced and laced with biblical allusions.

With the use of a specialized vehicle that included a battering ram, the FBI resorted to spraying CS gas into the complex in an effort to force Koresh out of the fortress. The Mount Carmel Center went up in flames during the advance; however, how it happened is still up for debate. Seventy-nine Branch Davidians died in the subsequent fire while barricaded inside the structure; 21 of these deceased were under the age of 16.

Koresh, 33 at the time, passed away from a head wound caused by a gunshot while the fire was still burning thus ending the House of David.

Chapter Conclusion

In previous chapters, we saw the effect a majority can have upon any group or collective. In this chapter, we learned about the sinister effect that a charismatic and vocal minority can have on the same group. In traditional Christian biblical texts, the Devil is presented as a metaphor for how attractive and pleasurable acts of evil can be when presented by a charismatic figure. Ignoring Christian principles, very often acts that the majority of us would consider as immoral occur because they are presented in a palatable manner by a figure we trust implicitly. The clear manipulation of the human psyche was present in all of the cult leaders presented in this chapter, and hopefully, the awareness of their modus operandus, as well as increased development of critical thinking among the general populace ensures that Jonestown never rises again.

Chapter 5: Organized Religions

If 13 years of Catholic School have taught me anything, it's that Jesus has a whole lot of rules for a man who went on boys' trips for the majority of his adult life. I had attended a church school since I was four years old, till I was 17 and in all that time, never have I felt the holy warmth of love and acceptance from anything other than a deep-dish pepperoni pizza.

The school I had gone to was a church school that only admitted me because my two older brothers had attended previously and they were going for a hat trick, but dodgy admission requirements aside, the school was well-known for being 1) an all-boys school, 2) one of the better local schools and 3) as catholic as an Irish bare-knuckle boxer. Every Friday, we were forced to sit through a two-hour-long Mass where a priest employed by the school would deliver sermons laced with spiritual wisdom such as "Puberty is the Devil's work," "God wants you to be good at Mathematics," and my personal favorite "Stop staring at the female teachers." Needless to say, they were doing the Lord's work. Everyday before the start of our morning lessons we would have a 45-minute-long religion lesson explaining the basics of Catholicism, simplified versions of biblical stories, and how there are very specific rules you need to follow if you don't want to suffer eternal damnation. Now, call this an uneducated guess, but telling groups of six-year-old children that their fates are condemned to sulfur and brimstone if they don't listen to your teachings is not great.

I distinctly remember one specific lesson when I was eight years old. We were learning about monotheism and polytheism, basically the difference between religions that worship a single God like the Abrahamic religions and religions that follow multiple deities like Hinduism. The teacher very patiently explained that while the other Abrahamic religions were similar to the catholic doctrine, they are different enough to be considered as non-believers and that when they die, they would go to purgatory for denying the existence of the one true God. Having been raised in a non-religious household, that Revelation (no pun intended) was terrifying. My mother was an atheist, did that mean she was going to hell? The only thing more terrifying than the damnation of my mother's soul, was the fact that all my classmates didn't seem too bothered by the knowledge that non-believers go to hell. It seemed perfectly reasonable to their little crayon-sniffing brains, their parents said the same thing after all.

During parent-teacher meetings, my teachers had expressed to my mother some worry that I hadn't fully absorbed the Christian spirit, which in hindsight sounds far more sinister than it did at the time. Apparently falling asleep during sermons, rolling my eyes at the sign of the cross, and calling Jesus a "30-year-old deadbeat who lived with his mum" wasn't very Catholic. Eventually, I reached the age where I had to start attending catechism lessons in preparation for my Confirmation. Now, I was not aware that I had to attend these lessons, it was only after one of my friends had informed me that a really pretty girl was in the same class as him that I suddenly became interested in the lessons. Many adults had praised my initiative in trying to find my faith and the consistency of my attendance. Who would have thought teenage hormones were capable of so much?

For the final part of my catechism lessons, I had to set up a meeting with my parish priest and convince him that I believed deeply enough to be a confirmed Christian. As I sat down with him, we had an hour-long discussion about faith and how it can change someone's life. He told me that faith is trusting what the Bible says even when it doesn't make sense. God is omniscient and thus knows what the right path to take is. All that his followers needed to do was follow the good book, and you'll be awarded paradise. Having faith isn't about thinking, it's about feeling. If I felt God's power flowing through me, then I would automatically know what the right choices to make in life would be and I would be supported by all my brothers and sisters in Christ.

To my regret, that speech made me a believer for a bit. Being a part of such a large seemingly supported community was the perfect way to sell religion to a lonely lost pre-teen. For the longest time, I chased what I thought was faith, and let scripture guide me. And I'm not ashamed to say that it felt good. So many people supported my decision to the point where I was convinced it was the right move to make. But as I grew older and gained an interest in history, I learned that throughout the ages, awful things had been committed in the name of faith. Things ranging from massively organized affairs like the crusades, to the more nuanced and subtle endeavors like their historical animosity towards the LGBTIQ+ community. When I became a teenager, like most of us, I started self-reflecting on the concept of responsibility and what consequences my actions would result in. I eventually came to the conclusion that if my choices had real effects in the material world, and I had the potential to affect those who are close to me, then I couldn't hide behind faith to guide my actions. We all live with the results of every decision we've made in our lives, in order to be fully satisfied with those results, we can't afford to be lazy and let a book written 2000 years ago make those decisions.

The idea that I would let an archaic and unintelligible piece of text dictate my life suddenly made no sense. Why in the world couldn't I eat shellfish? What was wrong with eating meat on Fridays? So many arbitrary rules exist within the text of the Bible which would never be implemented today. And the individuals who specifically prepare to interpret those texts and apply them to church-goers have, historically, used their platform to commit countless atrocities throughout history, all in the name of faith.

The philosopher Albert Camus inspired this view of religion. To Camus, existence is simply a series of nonsensical events strung together by the universe known as the Absurd. In order to fully accept and affirm their own uncomfortable existence, they needed to focus on what occurs in this life as opposed to acting in a way that would let them enter a theoretical paradise afterward. Looking at things from a pragmatic perspective, an afterlife, while nice, is purely hypothetical to anyone who isn't dead. But life is a certainty for anyone who has ever existed. From an existential perspective acting in a way that would prioritize the potential reality for actual reality is immensely unwise. From an ethical perspective, any good deed accomplished in the interest of getting into paradise was done with the express desire for a reward, the eternal reward. What moral virtue can come out of actions motivated by self-interest? If Christian dogma compels someone to act in a particular way, then it can be deduced that if that motivation is removed then the person wouldn't act in that way. That's not a morally good person. That is an extorted person.

Religious Indoctrination

Indoctrination is defined as "The process of inculcating a person with ideas, attitudes, cognitive strategies or professional methodologies." This is often accomplished by placing an individual in an environment reminiscent of an echo chamber, such as community events or political rallies. In this case, it would be religious education centers like Catechism and church schools in the case of Catholicism. An echo chamber is an environment where similar opinions or sentiments are repeatedly communicated with very little to no opposition to them.

In a sense of the word, this is a type of informational influence, especially when coming from a source whom an individual holds as an esteemed authority on the way reality should be perceived such as a surrogate brother figure or the parish priest. The source is deemed to know more than the individual receiving the information and thus, the individual internalizes whatever behaviors they witness from the source and amend their own thoughts and behaviors in order to mirror the source better. When individuals are young, they are ignorant of what correct behaviors should consist of. That is why babies often mimic their parents and toddlers use phrases similar to those used by their caretakers. When individual children perceive "important" acts in a particular way, they assimilate that behavior remarkably quickly. If they are then placed in an environment where that kind of behavior and thinking is encouraged, then the assimilation occurs quicker due to positive reinforcement confirming their decision that certain behavior is not only encouraged, but is rewarded.

Additionally, normative social influence is a factor that cannot be ignored. When an individual lives in a community with uniform beliefs, being an outlier may result in social ostracism. That would therefore result in a greater likelihood of individuals publicly complying with the norms and rules of the group in order to maintain a social relationship with other individuals.

Americans are still debating whether or not religion should be taught in public schools. While the topic of religious discussions in the classroom doesn't garner as much media attention as it used to, it is nevertheless a crucial point of contention in the larger debate over the place of religion in public life. The more religious folk among the population believe that banning the school-sponsored religious practice is a state effort to keep God and religion out of public schools. Such an endeavor, they believe, violates the First Amendment's guarantee of the freedom to practice one's faith.

Their counterparts worry that conservative Christians and similar parties are trying to force their ideals on pupils who may not necessarily wish to follow the same customs. They note that federal courts have routinely held that governmental support of liturgy and the majority of other religious practices in public schools violates the First Amendment banning the practice of religion by public schools.

The Supreme Court ruled in Cantwell v. Connecticut (1940) and Everson v. Board of Education of Ewing Township (1947) that the Establishment Clause and Free Exercise Clause of the First Amendment applied to the states. They state, "*Congress shall make no law respecting an establishment of religion or prohibiting the free exercise thereof.*" The Supreme court proceeded to deal with religious conservatives with a succession of significant blows beginning in the 1960s. Beginning with the famous Engel v. Vitale decision from 1962, which held that school-sponsored prayer, even nonsectarian prayer, infringed on the Establishment Clause. Since then, the Supreme Court has advanced, from forbidding school-sponsored prayer services at high school sporting events in

2000 and banning School-organized Bible study sessions promoting religious and moral education in 1963.

The court has often emphasized that the Constitution forbids public schools from indoctrinating students in religion in these and other rulings. However, defining just what indoctrination or school-sponsored religious activities can be challenging. Other constitutional protections complicate the situation. For instance, the First Amendment also safeguards the rights to free speech and association. In an effort to encourage student religious discourse and to get school support and funding for student religious organizations, religious groups have claimed these guarantees. However, there may be instances where other safeguards, including the right of pupils to be free from harassment, interfere with a student's or student club's freedom to express or participate in religion on school grounds.

In one instance, a federal appeals court, for instance, upheld a high school's decision to forbid a student from donning a T-shirt with a biblical scripture against homosexuality. In other instances, certain student religious organizations want the freedom to remove pupils who do not adhere to their philosophies. For instance, the Christian Legal Society (CLS), which has branches at several law schools, demands that people who hold leadership roles sign a statement renouncing "unbiblical activities," such as having sex outside of heterosexual marriage. The organization proceeded to open lawsuits against a number of colleges since the latter claimed that such a policy ran counter to their nondiscrimination policies. The Supreme Court decided against CLS in one of these cases, holding that these nondiscrimination measures were legal as long as they were impartial in terms of point of view and applied equally to any and all organizations seeking recognition on campus.

The courts have made a clear distinction between privately funded religious speech by students and publicly supported religious oration, such as blessings by an invited priest at a commencement ceremony. In Lee v. Weisman (1992), the Supreme Court clarified the fact that a clergyman's blessing at a state school gathering would be in violation of the separation of religion and state. When school authorities work with children to create student-delivered religious teachings, judges typically come to the same conclusion. However, when students take independent action to incorporate a religious statement or prayer at a school ceremony or other comparable event, federal courts are more split. By highlighting the private roots of this type of religious expression, several courts have sustained the validity of student-initiated religious speech.

In its rulings on officially sanctioned religious expression in schools, the Supreme Court has consistently drawn a distinction between "teaching about religion," which is legally valid and educationally appropriate, and religious activities like prayer or Bible studies, which are intended to instill religious sentiments and values. One of the more well-known conflicts between church and state is the conflict between Darwin's theory of evolution, which explains the creation of species through evolution by means of natural selection, and Creationism, the belief that life originated as it is depicted in the creation story of Genesis, who's proponents believe life is too intricate to have appeared without divine providence.

Courts have also devoted a lot of time and effort to the deliberation of permitting Bible study programs in public schools. The teaching of the Bible as literature is sometimes permitted by the Supreme Court, although other school districts have put in place Scripture study curricula that authorities have ruled unconstitutional. Judges have frequently come to the conclusion that these programs are blatant attempts to spread one specific interpretation of the Christian Bible. These Bible study programs are typically deemed unlawful by courts because, in their opinion, they present the Bible as doctrine or are intended to instill certain religious beliefs. It would take critical readings and literary criticisms of the text rather than devotional readings for a public classroom to potentially study the Bible without going against constitutional restrictions.

Not every instance of religion being taught in schools involves advancing the beliefs of the majority. Christian organizations have explicitly raised objections, claiming that by fostering cultural tolerance, educational practices discriminate against Christianity. In one instance, the U.S. Court of Appeals took into account a New York City Department of Education guideline governing the kinds of emblems that may be shown throughout different religious festival seasons. The department allowed the exhibition of solely secular Christmas symbols, such as a Christmas tree; it expressly restricts the presentation of a Christmas nativity scene in state education. However, the agency allows the display of a menorah as a sign for Hanukkah and a star and crescent to recall Ramadan (Hernández, 2009).

In a different well-known case, Citizens for a Responsible Curriculum successfully argued against a health education curriculum that covered sexual orientation in Montgomery County Public Schools in 2005 (Citizens for a Responsible Curriculum et al v. Montgomery County Public Schools et al, 2005). The teacher's manuals for the Montgomery County syllabus contained elements that criticized some religious views on homosexuality as having theological flaws and compared such views with what the manual depicted as the more agreeable and accepting perspectives of some other faiths. The district court came to the conclusion that the curriculum promoted some faiths while demeaning those of others, both intentionally and unintentionally. The county revised these teaching resources to exclude any mention of specific religious beliefs, making it more challenging to effectively refute them in court because the teachings did not criticize or celebrate any one religious tradition.

Chapter Conclusion

Spiritual leaders are supposed to be beacons of virtue and shepherds to their flock. With that responsibility comes a great ability to incite and rally mobs. Take the Westboro Baptist Church in Kansas. Led by Pastor Fred Phelps, the WBC is a hate group/echo chamber of homophobic, antisemitic, and racist preaching where violence, hate, and anger towards these minorities are encouraged by the church. Preaching such vitriolic filth from their mouths, this small church spreads nothing but suspicion and bad faith among its members, inciting and inflaming their existing prejudices to dangerous proportions. Religious apologists may argue that they aren't affiliated with any official branch of the Christian religion, but the fact that they can still use the Christian faith to do harm is enough to place partial responsibility at the feet of organized religion.

That being said, not all of the blame can be placed at the feet of organized religions. If there was only ever a single source of problems, then solutions would come far easier. Another major problem is the believers themselves. The Bible compares Jesus and his apostles to shepherds while the believers are compared to sheep to be led. While that may be an affirmation by the church to be responsible guides to their congregation, it also perpetuates a lack of agency from believers. The metaphor of "sheeple" can only go so far without infantilizing and justifying unacceptable behavior from believers. People who can be swayed by a little bit of charisma and a lack of awareness of their internal biases aren't thinking, moral people, they become little more than an instrument of a higher power, which is quite ironic in the grand scheme of things.

That all being said, this is not a condemnation of Christianity. There has been a multitude of good Christians who have dedicated their lives to the service of others and live the nobler lives that any of us could fathom. The same can be said for multiple individuals who follow different religions. There have been multiple individuals of varying religious beliefs who have toiled and struggled for humanity through either philanthropic charity work or the development of new and innovative concepts for the betterment of mankind. These remarkable individuals are just that, however. Individuals. While many of them may be motivated by the more altruistic tenants of their faith, they are not acting on behalf of the institutions they follow. Many organized religious organizations have the resources and ability to carry out good in the world, but very few institutional projects of significance have been actioned. Lip-service and empty words seem to be the main export of our religious leaders, and as the representatives of the faithful, that cannot be acceptable.

The majority of religious texts have fables of religious leaders acting by example and being the outlier of virtue surrounded by sin and apathy to the downtrodden. While acts of service equivalent to those described in scripture may seem unrealistic to the average person, the responsibility of spiritual leaders of every religion is to live and breathe dogma. When you dedicate your life to the pursuit of divinity and its teachings, then the responsibilities of such a choice must also be on your shoulders. As stated earlier, we must carry the consequences of all our decisions, because no one, least of all an ineffable biblical figure of dubious activity, can carry them for us. If an individual chooses to pursue the path of a spiritual leader, they must do all they can to uphold the values of the scripture they preach to their flock.

Chapter 6: Support of Corrupt Governments

Since the Nixon administration and the notorious Watergate scandal, there has been an increase in global awareness of the damaging effects that political corruption has on both economic growth and confidence in democratic political systems. When an individual placed in a position of trust by constituents leads to the said individual using their position for their own personal gain, that person has betrayed the goodwill of the people and should be held accountable for their actions. In the past couple of decades, public outcry has successfully led to the permanent impeachment of heads of state, the resignation of high-ranking officials, and the total reorganization of the cabinet. However, the fact that numerous politicians with spotty reputations continue to find success in winning office at the highest levels, like Italy's Silvio Berlusconi, who was elected Prime Minister multiple times, has received much less attention from the international press, despite the fact that such events have been highlighted as turning points in the fight against corruption.

There has been a rise in research on corruption during the past decades. This is partly due to a shift in perspective that occurred in the early 1990s in the United States as well as other important industrial nations. Trade liberalization and privatization have never had a better chance to spread throughout the world thanks to the fall of centralized economic policies in the former Soviet Union and the abandoning of the widely used socialist economic policies. To do this, it was necessary to protect capital and portfolio investments—which were largely flowing from developed nations—against conventional forms of government corruption. In other words, it was essential that corruption be significantly decreased due to the altered geopolitical and economic circumstances. As a result, organizations like the World Bank and the IMF started implementing anti-corruption policies in their dealings with state parties.

A significant portion of World Bank-sponsored research in this area is concerned with good governance in general. The main premise of the World Bank research is that a large portion of corruption is caused by ineffective government management, especially within the economic system. It follows that encouraging well-intentioned administrative improvements might significantly reduce corruption. High levels of corruption erode public and interpersonal trust, inhibiting civic behavior and group action, which can have disastrous effects on the continued existence of a political system. This problem is particularly problematic for new democracies and leads to a rise in support for authoritarian alternatives.

Seligson also discovered even more convincing statistical proof that corruption harms civil society ties, interpersonal trust, and political legitimacy of democracy in his analyses of several South American states His findings, which showed that individuals in high-corruptibility countries have more hostile opinions toward government workers than citizens in industrialized countries, were supported by Anderson and Tverdova. However, surprisingly, they discovered that in such nations, unfavorable opinions are unlikely to be held by those who support the government, which may help to explain how corrupt governments are able to hold onto authority in the midst of incessant controversy and subpar performance.

Clientelism

The fact that several state leaders are voted into office regardless of their less than straight-laced reputation is something that many of these studies tend to ignore, even though they have made a significant contribution to identifying both country-specific and transnational variables that fuel corruption or citizens' alienation from the political system. A corrupt transaction is one in which private parties and public figures exchange products for their personal financial benefit at the expense of the state as a whole. Government officials misusing their position of authority to demand bribes from residents and companies in order to gain public goods is one end of the spectrum. Kleptocracy, which occurs when political leaders, who are often autocrats, openly utilize governmental institutions to profit themselves in whatever manner imaginable, is the most severe example of this sort of corruption.

Instead, it is private individuals and businesses pulling the strings of these puppets that are engaging in corrupt behavior through the payment of bribes to officials in order to influence the outcomes of directives, legislative decisions, administrative regulations, and court rulings in their favor. Such unlawful actions may be taken to alter current policies or to influence future ones. Clientelism is typically described as an unofficial partnership between two parties with unequal socioeconomic power, where the financial benefactor has the upper hand since they have control over the resources that the client seeks for but frequently cannot obtain on their own. Consequently, it is a system that frequently creates a relationship of dominance and exploitation that sustains the iron grip that shrewd political leaders have on their consolidated power.

Clientelism also comprises reciprocal exchanges in the form of self-contained and advantageous trades of favors of disproportionate value, such as influential individuals gaining lucrative employment prospects, monetary contributions, and other, more fundamental resources in exchange for backing or votes. Clientelism is a phenomenon in politics that is founded on unofficial but generally recognized social, cultural, and behavioral standards. Modern patterns can be more anonymous and are often organized by party machinery awarding favor on behalf of the supporter. Traditional patterns are centered on individualized connections based on loyalty and reverence. There is strong evidence that clientelism thrives in societies where resources are constrained and governed by powerful political cliques. As a result, individuals are eager to trade their votes for any benefits they can muster.

According to one school of thinking, party lists common in proportional representation systems with big voting districts are more likely to be connected to corruption than in electoral systems with smaller districts and more direct competition between candidates. This line of reasoning is predicated on the idea that under the latter scenario voters have a better opportunity to hold individual politicians accountable, which aids in discouraging corruption. A more complex and subtle interpretation was offered by a second opposing school of thought, which claimed that the important factor is whether the voting system encourages politicians to seek a "personal vote," which would be more likely to culminate in decreased accountability, increased rent-seeking tactics, and possibly increased corruption.

Another series of research has attempted to explain the tactics used by politicians that rely on broad and well-managed clientelistic networks to win elections. According to Medina and Stokes' theory, incumbents who have a monopoly on political and economic resources are highly adept at maintaining the status quo in their favor by making serious threats against clients who could support the challenger, thus limiting electoral competition. Additionally, politicians have an incentive in maintaining economic stagnation and avoiding the establishment of wealth redistribution on more impersonal, merit-based principles that escape their control since poverty feeds the need for clientelistic handouts.

The winning election approach of incumbent candidates in the African nation of Benin disregards making pledges on programming forums. Instead, they deliver some of the assured favors before an election, which is viewed as more reliable than what their political adversaries are capable of providing. Clientelistic networks have proven to be particularly effective in Argentina in swaying the votes of the underprivileged and uneducated through the distribution of freebies. In addition to being highly successful at winning people's votes in exchange for material gifts, politicians in Argentina also have very good tools for keeping tabs on their supporters' ballots, which discourages them from defecting. In Argentina, clientelistic party tactics prioritized indecisive voters above ardent followers, contrary to what was traditionally believed.

In contrast to more rich and educated residents, Kitschelt observed that the less financially stable citizens with fewer educational opportunities are less invested in politicians who pledge long-term public benefits instead of personalized ones. Furthermore, the negative aspects of their customer position don't really bother the impoverished. They have immediate fundamental demands that must be met. Since they have been disregarded for many generations, they are aware that governmental schemes likely to assist them are unfeasible because these institutions do not function and are typically run by political bosses who control clientelist networks, which puts them right back where they started. This may be one of the reasons why clientelism may endure and thrive in the face of competitive elections. So long as inequality and poorly educated citizens exist, so does the opportunity for clientelism.

A growing volume of empirical material demonstrates the connection between clientelism and weak governmental institutions. What then characterizes effective governance institutions? Legal systems that preserve the rule of law and personal liberty are typically associated with strong institutions, as are administrative projects that deliver public products and services in an effective, fair, and timely fashion, with few and predictable corporate governance issues, and with minimal levels of governmental and bureaucratic corruption. Robust government institutions also include sufficient checks and balances that maintain a reasonable level of accountability in the policy-making process and hold elected officials responsible for their actions. On the other hand, whenever government bodies are ineffective and unable to deliver social infrastructure as they should, clientelism flourishes.

Clientelistic public officials have a strong interest in maintaining corrupt, inefficient, and burdensome government institutions since this position strengthen their credibility with low-income voters as the real issue solution. Corrupt politicians can present themselves as the most capable clown in the circus when the institutions are ineffective, political accountability is minimal, and the policy-making process is hidden from the public's view. In new democracies, Keefer discovered empirical data pointing to a substantial correlation between patronage politics and poor governmental institutions. Weak government entities are unable to offer public goods according to fair and reasonable standards because they frequently fall under the control of power groups that utilize them to grant favors and foster rent-seeking that benefits their clientele.

Since people are well aware that such pledges won't be kept, politicians cannot make convincing pre-election manifesto pledges based on a defined platform in such a situation. As a result, the only pledges that have any chance of being kept are those where candidates have a history of restricting the distribution of what are in essence public goods to their own constituencies for the promise of election. The primary reason why people choose to back corrupt governments is the interaction between the failure of government entities to provide public goods, on the one hand, and the capacity of clientelistic structures to profit from such a scenario, on the other.

Citizens may support corrupt governments because of the opportunities they offer, in spite of their corruption, if they are better equipped to grant favors. There are many instances of this type of thing happening, and some politicians have been brazening enough to confess it. Adhemar de Barros, one of Brazil's most significant politicians from the 1930s through the 1960s, is a well-known example. His followers used to proclaim, "He steals, but delivers!" We contend that individuals living in such situations are less inclined to penalize governments that they believe to be corrupt because weaker state institutions provide fertile cultivation grounds for clientelistic politics to fester in.

On the other hand, in places where government institutions are strong, we see that the rule of law and property rights are upheld by an effective legal system, a government bureaucracy that provides public goods in a competent and perfunctory manner, effective economic regulatory requirements, and responsibility and openness standards that monitor the actions of elected officials. Because of this, the ability to collect big clientele by manipulating the government is limited, and it is very expensive for both lawmakers and regular residents to distribute commodities privately. This makes it challenging for dishonest politicians to use clientelistic networks to purchase support in nations with robust democratic institutions. Crooked officials are much more likely to face public retribution in these institutional settings.

Scholars provide a variety of theories for the variance in corruption among nations, in addition to the prevalence of clientelism. Some relate varying electoral or political structures to varying degrees of corruption, equating federalism and presidentialism to higher levels of corruption and associating decentralization and single majority elections to lower levels of corruption. A society's acceptance of corruption may be explained by factors other than institutional ones, according to some academics, such as hereditary or cultural characteristics. Others contend that nations may fall into a cycle where the only candidates on the table are corrupt officials. Brazil serves as an illustration of this stereotype since it has traditionally had significant levels of corruption, a problem that has continued despite the democratization and consolidation that have occurred since the mid-1980s.

Information Hypothesis

The information hypothesis reveals one of the likely causes of ongoing public support for organizations that are clearly corrupt. A significant concern, especially in medium and low-income democracies, is poor resource management and increased politicization of the media, which makes efforts to conceal corruption more likely to be effective. Voters cannot reject crooked candidates if they are unaware of the corruption. Voters may dismiss claims of corruption even after they become public, especially if they come in the form of partisan accusations driven by political motivations. Voters should be anticipated to stop supporting corrupt politicians whenever detailed, reliable, and easily accessible information on corruption becomes available, assuming electoral support for kleptocrats is due to a lack of knowledge.

Voters should be anticipated to stop supporting corrupt politicians whenever detailed, reliable, and easily accessible information on corruption becomes available, assuming public support for corrupt governments is due to a lack of knowledge.

The information hypothesis is predicated on in a lot of cross-country literature on the institutional determinants of corruption. Voters would "punish a government for any increases in the perceived level of corruption compared to the level of corruption under the previous government," according to Margit Tavits. According to Alicia Adserá, Carles Boix, and Mark Payne, if citizens have ways to hold politicians responsible, corruption would decline when information is made more widely available. Unfortunately, a new wave of laboratory and field studies have shown conflicting results on this particular hypothesis.

Voters may dismiss complaints of corruption even after they become public, especially if they come in the guise of partisan political accusations. In rural India, for instance, a field trial reveals that a PR campaign on the expenditures of corruption has little impact on either polling numbers or the support candidates enjoy at the polls.

Insider-Outsider Theory

Another potential source of understanding into what is for some a highly vexing event is the Insider-Outsider Theory put forth by Eric Chang and Nicholas Kerr. They contend that when voters have an instrumental or identification tie with the incumbent, they are less inclined to penalize dishonest politicians at the polls. The idea that insiders enjoy a privileged treatment from the incumbent and, as a result, a variety of excludable commodities, is at the heart of the insider-outsider dichotomy.

This preferential access in turn shapes insiders' views and behavior differently from outsiders. They notably point to cost-benefit instrumentality and emotional identification as two important ways voters might identify with the incumbent. Affective identification refers to voters' shared sense of affinity for the incumbent, whereas cost-benefit instrumentality refers to voters gaining concrete advantages from the incumbent. They distinguish between two categories of insiders founded on these two mechanisms: While identification insiders indicate people who share the incumbent's party or ethnic allegiance, patronage insiders are those who are a member of the incumbent's patronage network.

It should be noted that the difference separating identity from instrumentality is theoretical and not always discernible experimentally. In fact, some people could fit into both categories. For instance, in Africa, co-ethnics are regularly patronized by other members of their own group, especially if the candidate actively does so. Insiders with a history of patronage may also be partisan allies of the incumbent. Because of this, we see both conceptions as ideal kinds that stand at opposing ends of a continuum, when in fact, insiders are more likely to place somewhere in the middle.

Citizens' emotional bonds to the incumbent as well as expectations of pecuniary rewards influence public views about corruption. One important factor in the creation of such an identity is partisanship. Partisanship is traditionally defined as a person's emotional commitment to a particular party that is based on a belief in a common identification with a social group. Voters who support the incumbent partisan ally may display partisan prejudice and believe that the incumbent is less corrupt than other candidates. Particularly, compared to other people, co-partisans are less likely to look for specific information on corruption affecting the incumbent. Furthermore, co-partisans are less inclined to embrace material that implicates their party since doing so would damage the party's positive uniqueness. Co-partisans are similarly prone to consider accusations of corruption against their political leading figures as attacks by rival groups or the media with political agendas.

Affective identity has the potential to shape citizens' tolerance for corruption as well as their perceptions of corruption. Both categories examine citizens' acceptance of people whose conduct they do not generally favor, hence Goren's research showing that partisanship influences one's moral tolerance is pertinent to our grasp of corruption tolerance. Co-partisans may be more tolerant of corruption charges affecting their incumbent than other voters due to partisan prejudice. Ethnic prejudice can also make members of the same group more understanding of their ethnic compatriots. In general, identity insiders may minimize their dislike of corruption because they place a higher importance on their social connections with the in-charge than on morality and the law. As a result, we anticipate identity insiders will be more tolerant of wrongdoing since their connection has changed how they view corruption.

Conceptual confusion is caused, in part, by the way corruption has been described or rather, inconsistently defined. One definition of corruption looks at public sentiment to decide what constitutes political malfeasance. Scaled according to elites' and the public's inclination to penalize political conduct, Arnold Heidenheimer categorizes corruption as white, gray, or black. Because behaviors that are publicly labeled as corrupt are by definition less acceptable, judgments of and capacity for abuse of power may even be seen as comparable. In contrast, John Garner and the legalist perspective assert that *"if an official's act is prohibited by laws established by the government, it is corrupt; if it is not prohibited, it is not corrupt even if it is abusive or unethical."* (Heidenheimer & Johnston, 2017)

Citizens' perception of corruption is measured by how strongly they think a political player is engaging in dishonest activities, according to Chang and Kerr. In contrast, a citizen's propensity to reject a political actor's involvement in the graft is shown by their tolerance for corruption. It is crucial to distinguish between perceptions of corruption and tolerance. Even while research has conclusively shown how negatively perceived corruption affects individuals' democratic values, it is conceivable that voter tolerance for corruption may also play a role in corruption. The corruption paradox can be understood better by differentiating between perceptions and tolerance since one can credibly explain voters' seemingly contradictory voting conduct to their varied attitudes toward corruption. Despite believing that corruption is pervasive, their study demonstrates that patronage insiders have higher degrees of tolerance for their dishonest clientele.

This draws a crucial theoretical distinction between how corruption is seen and how it is tolerated, and it particularly contends that these two distinct attitudes toward corruption alter depending on whether a person is a political insider or outsider. Patronage network participants see higher levels of corruption and are more accepting of it than outsiders. Furthermore, those who are artisanally or racially connected to the incumbent are far less likely to believe that corruption is a prevalent problem. Additionally, the insider-outsider concept sheds light on the conundrum of why voters detest corruption yet keep electing corrupt leaders. The key message is that how voters perceive corruption and behave during elections depends significantly on whether they are insiders or outsiders. The idea of reverse causality, or if those with greater perceptions of corruption could seek out patronage relationships to build ties with powerful people rather than using legal procedures to resolve issues, might be a genuine cause for worry. Although persons with high views of corruption may find it sensible to rely on prominent people, doing so may be challenging because conflict resolution is a restricted service provided at the influential person's discretion. As was previously said, citizens who are already committed to a long-term, mutually beneficial connection between the citizens and the prominent person are frequently the only ones allowed to solve problems.

Chapter Conclusion

When we look at the leaders shepherding our peers and fellow constituents today, the stench of sleaze and dirty money permeates the air like cigarette smoke in a mafia movie. But linking back to the sentiments expressed in the previous chapter, we not only have to ensure accountability in our political and religious leaders, but in ourselves too. Denying the existence or benevolence of an incorporeal omnipotent father figure in the sky is wasted if you just change him out for a bleached teeth Harvard legacy with more oil in his hair than the Gulf of Mexico. Keeping our representatives accountable and transparent means actively watching their actions and ensuring that they remain in line with the well-being of their constituents as opposed to themselves.

Chapter 7: Cancel Culture and Other Forms of Ostracism

Ostracism was described as a democratic process used by Ancient Greek Athenians that allowed any citizen to be exiled from the city-state of Athens for 10 years. Ostracism was frequently utilized as a preventative measure, even if there were cases where the public's hostility toward the citizen was evident. It was employed to deal with those that the state perceived as threats or prospective tyrants; however, in many cases, popular opinion influenced the decision, nonetheless. The term "ostracism" is still often used to describe many types of social rejection. Today, it is a tactic used to isolate nonconformists from the rest of society, whether it is justified or not.

Historical Context

Historically, the procedure in Ancient Greece required the will of the majority in order to action Ostracism. In the assembly, the Athenians were questioned on their desire to organize an ostracism ceremony each year. The name of the person to be shunned was written on pottery shards in a part of the agora that had been set aside and properly barred by the inhabitants, many of whom were illiterate. To ensure that the votes remained secret, the shards were stacked face down. If a quorum was met, the individual whose pile held the most shards would be exiled. If at least 6,000 votes were cast in total, the ostracism was regarded as legitimate.

Ten days were given to the nominee to flee the city. The punishment for trying to go back was death. There was no forfeiture of position or confiscation of the expelled man's possessions. He was permitted to return after 10 years without being stigmatized, with earlier returns permitted in cases of emergency like the Persian Invasion. Ostracism was clearly distinct from other systems of Athenian law; it did not include an accusation and the individual being banished had no chance to provide a defense. The two phases of the procedure were carried out in the opposite sequence from that of practically every trial system; in this case, it was as if the jury was first asked, "Would you like to condemn anyone?," followed by, "Whom do you desire to implicate?"

Ostracism did not serve a single, overarching aim since it was practiced by countless individuals throughout many decades amid a changing political climate and cultural landscape. Both the results and the original intent that it was conceived may be divined by tracking its development throughout history.

People who were shunned for the first time during the decade following the first Persian invasion's failure were all connected to or related to the despot Peisistratos, who had ruled Athens. His family took sanctuary with the Persians once his son Hippias was overthrown with Spartan assistance. Nearly 20 years later, Hippias arrived at Marathon with their invading army. The nascent democratic government in Athens faced the twin perils of tyranny and Persian aggression, and both were met with ostracism.

In Athens, conflicts amongst territorial and political groups centered around politicians gave rise to tyranny and democracy. In response, the democracy worked to lessen the prominence of parties as the object of citizen loyalty in many aspects of its design. Ostracism may have also been meant to serve the same purpose by temporarily removing a party from power in order to help diffuse conflicts that endangered the State's order. Ostracism appears to have been utilized in later decades, when the prospect of tyranny was less imminent, to choose between dramatically divergent policies. Individual voters' motivations cannot be ascertained. The candidates may just have been someone the submitter loathed and voted for out of personal vengeance.

In order to provide a safe haven or release for those harboring primitive resentments and desires or political objectives, ostracism rites could have additionally been an attempt to deter people from secretly killing or assassinating unacceptable or rising leaders. According to Gregory H. Padowitz's theory, "ostracism" would then be the appropriate response to murder, which would ultimately be to everyone's advantage as the unfortunate person would live and have a shot at redemption and civilization would be able to wash out the bad taste of feuds, civil war and murder from its palette.

Ostracism Today

Without necessarily necessitating "acts of verbal or physical abuse," Kipling Williams defines ostracism as "*any act or acts of ignoring and excluding an individual or groups by an individual or a group.*" Today, the exile or shunning of a person from society would be considered inhumane so Williams hypothesizes that modern forms of shunning most frequently include types of silent treatment, which is the intentional refusal to communicate with someone in a passive-aggressive manner. Particularly with electronic communication, it is rather simple to use silent treatment such as "unanswered messages" or "ignored emails." The basic human wants of connection, identity, autonomy, and meaningful existence are regarded as being threatened by being shunned on social media, especially by individuals who grew up during the social media boom. Cyber-ostracism (being ignored or receiving fewer manifestations of positive reinforcement) has caused more prosocial behavior among the digital generation, which should not be confused with cyber-rejection (actively receiving "dislikes," rude comments on a profile, etc.), which has caused a greater threat to the need for belonging and self-esteem and could potentially lead to social withdrawal.

Additionally, public ostracism is one of the more common attitudes that the general public directs towards whistleblowers. An individual, frequently an employee, who divulges information about conduct inside a private or public organization that is seen to be unlawful, immoral, illegitimate, dangerous, or fraudulent is known as a whistleblower. Whistleblowers can provide information or accusations through a number of private or public avenues. A whistleblower may also make allegations public by speaking with other groups like the press, the state, or police departments. Both the public and commercial sectors are susceptible to whistleblowing. Some consider whistleblowers as altruistic martyrs for the general good and corporate responsibility, while others label them as "backstabbers" or "defectors." It still carries with it cultural implications of treachery, ranging from "denunciations" on one level to "snitching" on another.

In *qui tam* proceedings, which allow accomplices in the

prosecution of another private individual to earn either partial or full pecuniary damages from the state, some even charge them with only seeking personal glory and fame or see their actions as driven by avarice. It's possible that many people don't even think about coming forward since they are afraid of being punished as well as of losing their connections with coworkers and other people. Employees in government, industry, and academics may become aware of significant environmental and health concerns, but corporate regulations may threaten individuals who disclose these early warnings with reprisal.

Employees of private companies, in particular, may run the danger of losing their jobs, getting demoted, not receiving promotions, etc. if they alert the relevant authorities to environmental hazards. Government personnel might also be in danger of alerting the public to health or environmental hazards, though this possibility may be less likely. There are instances of "early warning scientists" being persecuted for alerting the public and government to unpalatable facts regarding imminent danger. Additionally, there have been instances where young scientists have been dissuaded from pursuing contentious scientific disciplines out of concern about harassment.

Cancel Culture

A term from the late 2010s and early 2020s known as "cancel culture" or "call-out culture" describes a sort of ostracism in which someone is ejected from social or professional circles, whether it be on the internet, on social media, or in real life. It is sometimes said to manifest itself in the form of shunning or boycotting a person (typically a celebrity) who is seen to have behaved or talked in an inappropriate way. Since late 2019, the expression "cancel culture" has been more common, most frequently as a realization that society will hold offenders accountable. Conservatives in the US have more recently started using the word as a shorthand to describe what they see to be excessive responses to politically incorrect statements.

The argument around cancel culture, according to a piece made by Harvard University professor Pippa Norris, is between those who claim that it offers marginalized groups a voice and others who claim that it is hazardous because it suppresses freedom of expression and/or the chance for open discussion. Norris underlines how social media has aided in the spread of the cancel culture.

On the one hand, it is debatable if this tactic is a viable means of organizing networked collectivity for underprivileged communities that lack the means to seek legal remedy or a public apology to accomplish social justice and cultural transformation. According to this perspective, "canceling" refers to a decision to turn away from a person or a thing that is seen as morally repugnant. For people who disregard what are seen as ethical norms, it is a type of societal pressure. It might be argued that influential public figures should be held responsible for their words and actions—or lack thereof—at a time of fast-shifting moral standards and increased cultural considerations around the building of social identities.

Conversely, both conservative and liberal opponents contend that the practice has become so pervasive, particularly on college campuses, that it now poses a danger to the traditional liberal principles of free expression and open discussion from a range of viewpoints. Critics warn that this is a slippery slope that would silence a range of controversial opinions. The process may begin with reasonable criticism of situations generating widespread moral censure, such as revealing serial sexual abusers. On college campuses, the approach may eventually stifle intellectual discussion, intellectual variety, and academic freedom by encouraging groupthink, undermining tolerance for contrarians, and highlighting the dangers of confirmation bias in social science.

The Spiral of Silence Theory, according to Norris, may be a factor in why people are reluctant to express their own views on social media platforms for fear of being reprimanded because their opinions, particularly those related to politics, are in violation of the norms and understanding of the majority group. The spiral of silence theory, as coined by Elizabeth Noelle-Neumann, states that a person's desire to communicate their own political beliefs is influenced by how they perceive the distribution of the general public's opinions. The key thesis is that social contact affects people's propensity to voice ideas. The theory states that when people see that their unique perspective is shared by everyone in the group, they will become more outgoing and secure in expressing it. However, if the person senses that the group does not share their perspective, they are more likely to be reticent and keep quiet. This is a self-expression act that has the power to alter the "global environment of opinion," altering how people perceive one another and their desire to voice their own thoughts. This, in turn, is a manifestation of the normative influence of a majority unto a minority.

However, it is important to note that Noelle-Neumann emphasized that the consequences are also likely to be unintended, where self-censorship results from a variety of social pressures for the unconventional to conform to the majority views, such as the fear of offending, the desire to avoid getting into a fight over contentious issues, and risk upsetting the group dynamic. On contentious, delicate, and divisive matters like those involving sex and sexuality, gender identity, sexism, racism, and ethnic or religious identities, caution against challenging the status quo is likely to be greatest.

Chapter Conclusion

In recent years, contentious discussions regarding the cancel culture have become more intense as a result of the widening ideological and value gaps that separate both sides of the political spectrum. Of course, the public exposure of heretics and those who stray from the beaten course is old hat, as seen by the zealous persecution of those who practice non-conformity in their religion, the medieval practice of hanging people at the gallows on the weekends, or the infamous Salem witch trials.

More political discourse than intellectual insight has been created by recent media conjecture concerning the "cancel culture" label's shaming of prominent public people in the fields of pop culture, literature, politics, as well as universities, and academia. However, if a cancel culture has developed in academia, as critics claim, from the justified criticism of allegedly inflammatory deeds and words to become a wave undermining tolerance for opposing views, limiting freedom of speech, and enforcing uniform beliefs among academics, administration staff, and students, then there are real reasons for concern. From a normative standpoint, cancel culture works to ostracize and socially shun individuals who have incongruent beliefs from the mainstream. While some opinions are harmful to the overall betterment of mankind, censoring them and publicly shaming them will not eliminate those opinions. It will allow them to fester and cultivate and strengthen the conviction of those who hold them. Canceling controversial figures is a short-term solution to a long-term issue and can only hold people accountable to a minor degree.

Conclusion

The notion of conformity is a fascinating and terrifying one. The ability to change another's opinions is undeniably valuable, especially when in positions of authority. Being a manager or a supervisor of a team would be astronomically easier if each person thought the same way you did and held the same attitude to work. Conformity may be beneficial in ways that preserve our culture in the same way that conformity ensures that people are aware of the right actions to take in various circumstances and the mistakes they must avoid.

But in the long run, conformity also eliminates those traits which make us unique since it is non-uniform. Conformity just prevents us from speaking up when it might genuinely help a circumstance or a choice. By refraining from challenging and debating the group leader's decisions only because other members of the group support them, we avoid potentially disastrous outcomes that we obviously wish to steer clear from.

Humanity is such a fascinating project being overseen by all of us as a collective. The ability to collaborate and make something bigger than ourselves is something that cannot be overlooked, but many people seem to be able to. That same complexity also allows us the luxury of nuance. And the nuance in the human experience is the statistical impossibility that allows each of us to be unique in our own intimate and distinct way. Intentionally abandoning that luxury is abandoning what it is to be human. To have a favorite spot to think, to have your own unique rituals in the morning, and to have a movie scene that speaks to you more than anyone else.

When you dance to the beat of your own drum, you ensure that you always dance to your favorite song.

Humans are wonderful pieces of complex and intricate machinery that have developed a sense of identity and self-awareness. But they are so much more than that. To call a human a complex machine is to call the planets "a bunch of big rocks." It was less than a century ago that people of color were considered to be lesser citizens in the United States, and 50 years later, an African American President was chosen by the American people. Humans have this incredible ability to learn from their mistakes and be better. And the first step to being better is recognizing there's a problem. But unfortunately, when there's a fire, you can't put it out from inside the house. In order to recognize our own shortcomings as a collective, we have to step away from the collective and have the nerve to question convention and right wrongs. To throw away that responsibility in favor of only being a nameless face in the crowd is an insult to sentience and humanity. Humans are incredible creatures when they are allowed to be themselves. Why be a sheep in a flock, nameless and forgotten, when you could be a ripple in the ocean?

References

Arch R. Everson v Board of Education of the Township of Ewing, et al., (1947) U.S. LEXIS 2959.

Baron, R. S., Vandello, J. A., & Brunsman, B. (1996). *The forgotten variable in conformity research: Impact of task importance on social influence.* Journal of Personality and Social Psychology, 71(5), 915–927. https://doi.org/10.1037/0022-3514.71.5.915

Bibb Latané, & Fink, E. L. (1996). *Dynamic social impact theory and communication: a symposium.* Oxford U.P.

Campbell, J. D., & Fairey, P. J. (1989). *Informational and normative routes to conformity: The effect of faction size as a function of norm extremity and attention to the stimulus.* Journal of Personality and Social Psychology, 57(3), 457–468. https://doi.org/10.1037/0022-3514.57.3.457

Chang, E. C. C., & Kerr, N. N. (2016). *An Insider-Outsider Theory of Popular Tolerance for Corrupt Politicians.* Governance, 30(1), 67–84. https://doi.org/10.1111/gove.12193

Citizens for a Responsible Curriculum v. Montgomery County Public Schools, Civil Action No. AW-05-1194 (D. Md. May. 5, 2005).

Darley, J. M., & Latane, B. (1968). *Bystander intervention in emergencies: Diffusion of responsibility.* Journal of Personality and Social Psychology, 8(4), 377–383. https://doi.org/10.1037/h0025589

Dubrow-Marshall, L., & Dubrow-Marshall, R. (2017, November 20). *How cult leader Charles Manson was able to manipulate his "family" to commit murder.* The Conversation. https://theconversation.com/how-cult-leader-charles-manson-was-able-to-manipulate-his-family-to-commit-murder-70961

Engel v. Vitale, 370 U.S. 421 (1962).

Fischer, P., Krueger, J. I., Greitemeyer, T., Vogrincic, C., Kastenmüller, A., Frey, D., Heene, M., Wicher, M., & Kainbacher, M. (2011). *The bystander-effect: A meta-analytic review on bystander intervention in dangerous and non-dangerous emergencies.* Psychological Bulletin, 137(4), 517–537. https://doi.org/10.1037/a0023304

Hernández, J. C. (2009, January 14). *Battle on Crèches in Schools Goes to City Hall. The New York Times.* https://www.nytimes.com/2009/01/14/education/14nativity.html

Heidenheimer, A. J., & Johnston, M. (2017). *Political corruption: concepts & contexts. Routledge.*

Hickey, E. W. (2003). *Encyclopedia of murder & violent crime* (p. 276). Sage Publications.

Jolly, N. (2019, April 25). 25 years after Waco: Looking back at how David Koresh built his following. Guide. https://www.sbs.com.au/guide/article/2019/04/25/25-years-after-waco-lookin-back-how-david-koresh-built-his-following

Kassin, S.M. (2013). *Social psychology.* Nelson Education.

Kelman, H. C. (1958). *Compliance, identification, and internalization three processes of attitude change.* Journal of Conflict Resolution, 2(1), 51–60. https://doi.org/10.1177/002200275800200106

Lee v Weissman, 505 U.S. 577 (1992).

Manzetti, L., & Wilson, C. J. (2007). *Why Do Corrupt Governments Maintain Public Support?* Comparative Political Studies, 40(8), 949–970. https://doi.org/10.1177/0010414005285759

Norris, P. (2021). *Cancel Culture: Myth or Reality?* Political Studies, 1–30. https://doi.org/10.1177/00323217211037023

NW, 1615 L. S., Suite 800 Washington, & Inquiries, D. 20036 USA 202-419-4300 | M.-8.-8. | F.-4.-4. | M. (2019, October 3). *Religion in the Public Schools.* Pew Research Center's Religion & Public Life Project. https://www.pewresearch.org/religion/2019/10/03/religion-in-the-public-schools-2019-update/

Smith, J. R., & Louis, W. R. (2009). *Group Norms and the Attitude-Behaviour Relationship.* Social and Personality Psychology Compass, 3(1). https://doi.org/10.1111/j.1751-9004.2008.00161.x

Winters, M. S., & Weitz-Shapiro, R. (2013). *Lacking Information or Condoning Corruption: When Do Voters Support Corrupt Politicians?* Comparative Politics, 45(4), 418–436. https://doi.org/10.5129/001041513x13815259182857

Wunrow, R. (2013). *The psychological massacre: Jim Jones and Peoples Temple: An Investigation – Alternative Considerations of Jonestown & Peoples Temple.*

Sdsu.edu. https://jonestown.sdsu.edu/?page_id=29478

U.S. Const. amend. I.